# THE BEST OF THE TASTES OF TAHOE

## AND RENO

**A Restaurant Guide & Restaurant Recipe Cookbook**

**Written and Compiled by Sonnie J**

ISBN # 0-934181-05-5

For John, Ruth, Colleen and Bonnie
The best of Tahoe

# Table of Contents

8

# RENO/TAHOE

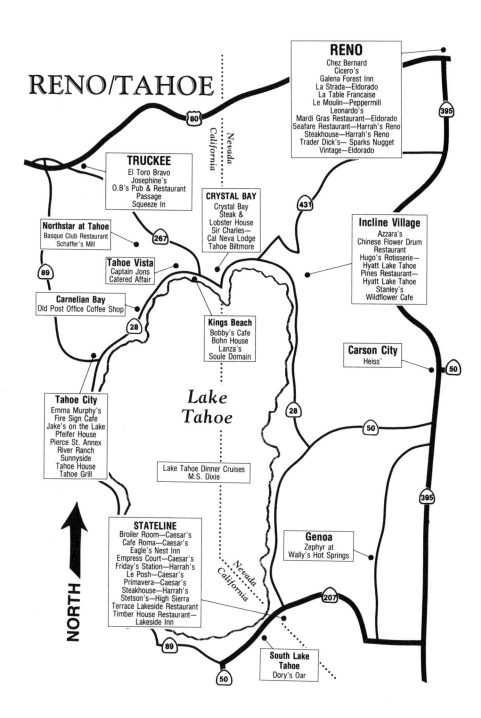

**RENO**
Chez Bernard
Cicero's
Galena Forest Inn
La Strada—Eldorado
La Table Francaise
Le Moulin—Peppermill
Leonardo's
Mardi Gras Restaurant—Eldorado
Seafare Restaurant—Harrah's Reno
Steakhouse—Harrah's Reno
Trader Dick's— Sparks Nugget
Vintage—Eldorado

**TRUCKEE**
El Toro Bravo
Josephine's
O.B's Pub & Restaurant
Passage
Squeeze In

**CRYSTAL BAY**
Crystal Bay
Steak &
Lobster House
Sir Charles—
Cal Neva Lodge
Tahoe Biltmore

**Incline Village**
Azzara's
Chinese Flower Drum
Restaurant
Hugo's Rotisserie—
Hyatt Lake Tahoe
Pines Restaurant—
Hyatt Lake Tahoe
Stanley's
Wildflower Cafe

**Northstar at Tahoe**
Basque Club Restaurant
Schaffer's Mill

**Tahoe Vista**
Captain Jons
Catered Affair

**Carnelian Bay**
Old Post Office Coffee Shop

**Kings Beach**
Bobby's Cafe
Bohn House
Lanza's
Soule Domain

**Carson City**
Heiss'

**Tahoe City**
Emma Murphy's
Fire Sign Cafe
Jake's on the Lake
Pfeifer House
Pierce St. Annex
River Ranch
Sunnyside
Tahoe House
Tahoe Grill

*Lake Tahoe*

Lake Tahoe Dinner Cruises
M.S. Dixie

**STATELINE**
Broiler Room—Caesar's
Cafe Roma—Caesar's
Eagle's Nest Inn
Empress Court—Caesar's
Friday's Station—Harrah's
Le Posh—Caesar's
Primavera—Caesar's
Steakhouse—Harrah's
Stetson's—High Sierra
Terrace Lakeside Restaurant
Timber House Restaurant—
Lakeside Inn

**Genoa**
Zephyr at
Wally's Hot Springs

**South Lake Tahoe**
Dory's Oar

California
Nevada

NORTH

13

**AZZARA'S**
930 Tahoe Blvd. (P.O. Box 3409)
Incline Village, NV 89450
(702) 831-0346
Hours: 5:00 p.m. - 10:00 p.m. Tuesday - Saturday
Credit Cards: Mastercard, Visa
Prices: Moderate
Reservations: None
Specialties: Italian

*If you've ever had an Italian friend whose mother cooked for you, you know what it's like to eat at Azzara's in Incline Village. It is a family place, a friendly place, a filling place. The extensive menu features all your Italian favorites, from pizza to lasagne (the best in town), to the surprise of Sam Azzara's daily specials. It is one of the most popular restaurants around because of its excellent food and comfortable atmosphere - a fine reputation has been made and Azzara's never lets you down, whether you're ordering a pizza out or settling in for an elegant full Italian feast. Casual attire is fine, and plan to get there early as they they line up at the door.*

# Fried Mozzarella Cheese

| | |
|---|---|
| 3 | eggs |
| | pinch of salt |
| 12 | slices mozzarella cheese |
| 4 | Tbsp. flour |
| 4 | Tbsp. fine bread crumbs |
| 1 | c. olive oil |

Beat eggs, add salt. Coat cheese slices with flour and dip them in beaten eggs. Roll in bread crumbs and dip again in beaten eggs. Fry in hot olive oil until cheese is golden brown. Drain and serve immediately.

*Serves 6*

# Funghi (Mushrooms with Garlic and Oregano)

| | |
|---|---|
| 1/2 | c. olive oil |
| 3 | cloves garlic, chopped |
| 3 | lbs. mushroom caps, cleaned and sliced |
| 1/2 | tsp. oregano |
| | salt to taste |
| 1 | Tbsp. Marsala wine |

In a large frying pan heat olive oil, add garlic and lightly brown. Add mushrooms. Sprinkle with oregano and salt to taste. Cook until mushrooms are tender, about 15 minutes. Marsala wine may be sprinkled on mushrooms while cooking for added flavor.

*Serves 6*

# Insalata Pomodori (Tomato Salad)

| | |
|---|---|
| 1 | head leafy romaine lettuce |
| 6 | large tomatoes, sliced |
| 1 | Tbsp. olive oil |
| 1/2 | tsp. oregano |
| 2 | Tbsp. fresh sweet basil, chopped |
| | salt and pepper to taste |

On a bed of leafy romaine lettuce, arrange the tomatoes. Sprinkle with olive oil, oregano and basil. Salt and pepper to taste.

*Serves 6*

# Sicilian Salad

| | |
|---|---|
| 1 | medium head iceberg lettuce |
| 1 | 2 1/4-oz. can olives, pitted and sliced |
| 2 | oranges, peeled and thinly sliced |
| 1/4 | c. salad oil or olive oil |
| 1/4 | c. orange juice |
| 2 | Tbsp. vinegar |
| 1 | tsp. salt |
| 1/2 | tsp. paprika |

Tear lettuce into small pieces and toss in salad bowl with olives and oranges. Make dressing by combining remaining ingredients. Add to salad.

*Serves 4 to 6*

# Pesto Sauce

| | |
|---|---|
| 2 | cloves garlic |
| 4 | bunches fresh basil leaves |
| 1 | Tbsp. toasted pine nuts |
| 4 | Tbsp. each Parmesan cheese, Pecorino romano cheese |
| 1 | c. olive oil |

Place first 4 ingredients in food processor. Slowly add the olive oil. This is sufficient sauce for 1 pound of spaghetti.

*Serves 3*

# Saltimbocca (Veal Scallopini with Ham)

| | |
|---|---|
| 12 | slices veal, thinly sliced |
| 12 | slices Prosciutto ham |
| 12 | sage leaves |
| 1 | Tbsp. butter |
| | salt and pepper |
| 1/2 | c. dry white wine (optional) |

On each veal slice, place a slice of Prosciutto ham and a sage leaf. Secure in place with a toothpick. Do not roll. Brown on both sides in butter for a few minutes. Salt and pepper to taste. Add wine. Reduce.

*Serves 6*

# Potato Gnocchi with Cheese

| | |
|---|---|
| 4 | lbs. potatoes, boiled |
| 4 | c. all-purpose flour |
| 1/2 | tsp. salt |
| 1/2 | lb. fontina cheese, sliced |
| 1/2 | c. butter |

Drain, cool and peel potatoes. Mash until smooth and dry. Add flour and salt and work into a dough. Break off pieces and roll into 1" long strips, about the thickness of a finger. Place on floured surface to prevent sticking. Bring large pan of salted water to a gentle boil and drop gnocchi in batches into water, removing them as soon as they float to the top, approximately 3 minutes. Alternately layer gnocchi and slices of fontina cheese in ovenproof casserole, sprinkling each layer with butter. Bake at 350, for 5 minutes and serve immediately.

*Serves 6*

# Sicilian Stuffed Baked Artichokes

| | |
|---|---|
| 4 | artichokes |
| | dash of lemon |
| 1 | c. Italian bread crumbs (parsley, bread crumbs, garlic, salt and pepper) |
| 2 | Tbsp. melted butter |

Cut off top and most of stem of artichokes. Boil in salted water with a dash of lemon until bottom of artichoke can be pierced easily with a fork. Cool at room temperature. Open leaves with your fingers and drop the bread crumbs down between the leaves. Drizzle melted butter between the leaves. Place in a casserole and bake at 500 for 10 minutes.

*Serves 4*

# Osso Buco

2        lbs. veal shanks, cut in 3" pieces
2        Tbsp. olive oil
2        Tbsp. flour
4        Tbsp. olive oil
1/2      c. dry white wine
1        14-oz. can Italian peeled tomatoes
         salt and pepper to taste
1        clove garlic, finely chopped
         grated rind of 1/2 lemon
3        sprigs parsley, finely chopped
1 - 2    anchovy fillets, finely chopped

Dip veal shanks in olive oil. Roll the shanks in flour and fry in olive oil. Brown evenly. Pour wine over veal and cook for 15 minutes. Add tomatoes and season with salt and pepper. Cover and cook over low heat for about 2 hours or until veal almost falls off bones. Spread Gremolada (recipe follows) on the veal a few minutes before serving and turn them once to distribute the flavors.

*Serves 4*

# Gremolada

1        clove garlic, minced
1        tsp. lemon rind, minced
1        Tbsp. parsley, minced
2        anchovy fillets, minced

Blend all ingredients together to make a paste.

# Veal with Red Wine Sauce

| | |
|---|---|
| 1/2 | c. butter |
| 1 | onion, finely chopped |
| 2 | lbs. stewing veal, boned and cut into pieces |
| | salt and pepper |
| 2 | c. red wine |
| 1 | c. chicken or beef stock, heated |
| 2 - 3 | sprigs parsley |
| 1 | large clove garlic, crushed |
| 1 | bay leaf |
| 1 | sprig thyme |
| 4 | tsp. flour |

Heat 3 oz. of the butter in a large casserole and saute onion until they begin to soften. Add veal and continue cooking until lightly browned, evenly. Season with salt and pepper to taste. Add wine and stock. Tie parsley, garlic, bay leaf and thyme together and add it to the casserole. Cover and continue to cook slowly over low heat for 1 1/2 hours or until veal is tender. Knead remaining butter with flour. Remove veal and place it on a hot platter and keep hot in low oven. Discard herbs. Slowly add kneaded butter to simmering sauce stirring constantly until it thickens. Pour sauce over the veal and serve at once.

*Serves 6*

# Turkey Breast with Mozzarella and Tomatoes

| | |
|---|---|
| 6 | Tbsp. butter |
| 6 | slices turkey breast, about 2 lbs. |
| | salt and pepper to taste |
| 6 | slices mozzarella cheese |
| 3 | large tomatoes, peeled and chopped |
| | fresh parsley, chopped |

Melt butter in large frying pan. Add turkey and fry until golden brown on both sides. Season with salt and pepper. Place turkey slices in shallow baking dish in 1 layer and cover each slice with a slice of mozzarella and some of the tomatoes. Dot with remaining butter and bake in moderate oven about 20 minutes or until tomatoes are cooked and cheese has melted. Sprinkle with parsley. (If you use cooked turkey, eliminate frying.)

*Serves 3 to 6*

# Chicken in Tomato and White Wine Sauce

| 1 | 3 1/2-lb. chicken |
|---|---|
| 4 | Tbsp. butter |
| 4 | Tbsp. olive oil |
| | salt and pepper to taste |
| 1/2 | c. dry white wine |
| 1 | lb. ripe tomatoes, peeled, seeded and pureed or |
| 1 | 1-lb. can Italian peeled tomatoes, pureed |

Cut chicken into 4 pieces. Heat butter and oil in a large pan. Brown chicken legs over high heat, then brown chicken breasts and wing sections. Season with salt and pepper. Lower heat and continue cooking until chicken is tender. Remove chicken from pan and keep warm. Stir wine into same pan and reduce. Add pureed tomatoes. Stir well and cook about 10 minutes. Return chicken pieces to pan and cook a few minutes longer. Serve immediately.

*Serves 4*

# Cassata Cake

| | |
|---|---|
| 1 3/4 | c. ricotta cheese |
| 2 | c. granulated sugar |
| 3 | Tbsp. water |
| | dash of ground cinnamon |
| 5 | squares bitter chocolate, crushed |
| 1 | lb. candied fruit |
| 4 | Tbsp. pistachio nuts, chopped |
| 1 | 1-lb. sponge cake |
| | few Tbsp. Maraschino liqueur |
| | confectioners' sugar |

Blend ricotta until smooth. Heat granulated sugar in water until lightly colored. Remove from heat and beat into ricotta. Add cinnamon, chocolate, half the candied fruit and the nuts to the mixture and blend thoroughly. Cut sponge cake in 1/2" thick slices and moisten in liqueur. Place a layer of cake in a deep round pan and spread ricotta mixture over it. Alternate with another layer of cake and ricotta, leaving layer of cake slices on top. Refrigerate overnight to set firmly. Carefully invert pan onto serving platter and gently remove pan so that cake remains in round shape. Decorate cake with remaining fruit and sprinkle with confectioners' sugar.

*Serves 12*

SONOMA COUNTY
## SAUVIGNON BLANC

PRODUCED & BOTTLED BY GRAND CRU VINEYARDS
GLEN ELLEN, CALIFORNIA USA — ALCOHOL 13.3% BY VOLUME

Lovely fruit aromas complemented by moderate oak flavors.  Medium-bodied with an elegant long finish.

An excellent choice to accompany shellfish, grilled fish, lightly curried foods and chicken.

# Basque Club
# Restaurant

**THE BASQUE CLUB RESTAURANT**
Northstar-at-Tahoe (P.O. Box 129)
Truckee, CA   95734
(916) 587-0260
Hours:  5:00 p.m. - 10:00 p.m. Thursday through Monday
winters only
Credit Cards:  American Express, Visa, Mastercard, Discover, Carte Blanch
Prices:  Moderate
Reservations:  Recommended
Specialties:  Traditional five-course Basque cuisine served
family style

*This is truly country-style food with home-style service - and the price is unbelievablly low for the amounts of food served in those big bowls.  Rustic yet elegant, with redwood panelling, candles, long tables, crisp white napery, windows overlooking the Northstar golf course - it is a juxtaposition of the rough and the smooth, the uptown and the farm.  The Basque Club Restaurant brings the locals back time after time - always a sign of exceptional food at good prices.  Try the paella - it's a special delight, even for gourmets.*

# Paella a la Behobie

| | |
|---|---|
| 1 | whole chicken |
| 1/2 | c. olive oil |
| 1 | large onion, chopped |
| 2 | red bell peppers, cut into strips |
| 4 | cloves garlic, minced |
| 1 | dozen clams or mussels or both, washed |
| 1 | dozen jumbo shrimp in shells |
| 2 | c. white rice |
| 1/2 | tsp. saffron |
| 3 | c. chicken stock or bouillon |

Cut chicken into 12 pieces. Brown chicken in olive oil. Add onion, peppers and garlic, saute for a few minutes. Add uncooked seafood, rice, saffron and chicken stock. Bring to boil, cover and cook until rice is done.

*Serves 12*

# Marinated Cornish Game Hen

6     20-oz. game hens
*Marinade:*
1     bottle white wine
8     oz. olive oil
1     bunch fresh thyme
3     sprigs fresh rosemary
1     clove garlic, pressed
3     Tbsp. honey
1/4   c. brown sugar
3     tsp. salt
2     Tbsp. paprika
2     tsp. cayenne pepper
1     c. prepared mustard
2     tsp. white pepper

Cut game hens into halves.  Mix all other ingredients in a pan.
Place hens into marinade and allow to marinate overnight.  Heat
oven to 325° F.  Place hens on tray and bake 25 to 35 minutes.
Game hens should be brown.  Marinade can be thickened by
reduction (see glossary) and used as a sauce with the game hens.

*Serves 12*

## Meet Me At
# BOBBY'S
### CAFE

**BOBBY'S CAFE**

**7900 North Lake Blvd. (P.O. Box 124, Crystal Bay, Nv. 89402)**

**Kings Beach, CA  95719**

**(916) 546-2329**

**Hours:  7:00 a.m. - 10:00 p.m. Daily**

**Credit Cards:  Mastercard, Visa, American Express**

**Prices:  Moderate**

**Reservations:  Not required**

**Specialties:  BBQ**

*Slow-cooked, barbecued specialties highlight the menu at Bobby's Cafe, on the corner of Highway 267 and North Lake Boulevard by the Woodvista Golf Course in Kings Beach. Chicken, Danish baby back ribs and beef ribs are marinated for 24 hours and then slowly cooked - tantalyzing smells! The barbecue dishes are served with garlic bread and a choice of two side dishes. It's a cozy cafe, cheery, and worth the stop on your way to and from skiing, beach or casinos. Breakfast offers a full line-up of omelette ingredients to "create your own." In the summertime at Bobby's, dine on the patio, the golf course is beyond and glimpses of the lake across the highway.*

# Barbecued Pork Tenderloins

| | |
|---|---|
| 20 | fresh tomatoes |
| 2 | yellow onions, finely chopped |
| 1 | Tbsp. oil |
| 1/4 | c. white wine |
| 2 | Tbsp. Worchestershire Sauce |
| 1/4 | c. white vinegar |
| | pinch cayenne pepper |
| 1/4 | c. molasses |
| 1/8 | c. brown sugar |
| 10 | drops Tabasco Sauce |
| | pinch of thyme |
| | pinch of dill weed |
| | pinch of tarragon |
| 2 1/2 | lbs. pork tenderloin |

Grate tomatoes in a food processor, set aside. Saute onions in oil. Combine all ingredients but pork and bring to a boil. Simmer 8 hours in covered stock pot. Wrap tenderloins in foil, cook 6 1/2 hours at 235° F. Marinate in warm sauce 24 hours. Slice pork in 1/4-inch thick slices. Reheat and serve.

*Serves 6*

# The Bohn House
## Fine Dining

**THE BOHN HOUSE**
8160 North Lake Blvd.
Kings Beach, CA  95719
Mailing address: P.O. Box 755
Carnelian Bay, CA 95711
(916) 546-5814
Hours:  5:30 p.m. - 10 p.m. Thursday - Monday
5:30 p.m.  Early-bird special
Closed Tuesday and Wednesday except during
holiday periods
Credit Cards:  American Express, Mastercard, Visa
Prices:  Moderate
Reservations:  Recommended
Specialties:  Continental Cuisine

*With years of restaurant experience behind them, Linny and Dick Bohn opened their classy little Kings Beach restaurant in early 1987 and began serving delectable dinners with a continental flair. The Bohn House is one of the places you know you must return to because each item on the menu calls to you and it is nigh to impossible to make up your mind. With its country French feel, and its indescribably delicious food, the Bohn House is a sophisticated addition to Lake Tahoe's North Shore dining. It is a particularly warm and comfortable establishment.*

# Frog Legs Saute Maison

| | |
|---|---|
| 10 | frog legs |
| | salt and pepper to taste |
| 1/2 | c. flour |
| 1/8 | c. olive oil |
| 1 | c. cooked rice |
| 1 | tsp. garlic, minced |
| 1/2 | c. white wine |
| 1/8 | c. lemon juice |
| 4 | oz. butter |

Season frogs legs with salt and pepper. Dust with flour. Saute in olive oil 5 to 7 minutes on medium-high heat. Place frog legs in ring of cooked rice. Add garlic to saute pan and cook 1 to 2 minutes on high heat. Add wine and lemon juice. Reduce. Remove from heat and add butter. Pour over frog legs and serve.

*Serves 2*

# Bohn House Salad Dressing

| | |
|---|---|
| 1 | c. olive oil |
| 1 | c. salad oil |
| 1 | c. red wine vinegar |
| 1 1/2 | Tbsp. dry English mustard |
| 2 | eggs |
| 1/8 | tsp. salt |
| 1/4 | tsp. white pepper |
| 1/8 | tsp. rosemary |
| 1/8 | tsp. thyme |
| 1/8 | tsp. oregano |
| 1/8 | tsp. sweet basil |

Blend all ingredients in a food processor, starting with liquid, then mustard, eggs and seasonings last.

*Makes 3 cups*

# Crepes Suzette

Crepe batter:
| | |
|---|---|
| 3 | c. milk |
| 1/4 | c. sugar |
| 3 | eggs |
| | gratings from 1/2 orange and 1/2 lemon |
| | flour |

Mix first 4 ingredients, adding enough flour to make a thin consistency. Pour thin layer of batter in small crepe pan. Turn once. Reserve while preparing sauce

Sauce:

| | |
|---|---|
| 1/2 | lb. butter |
| 1/2 | c. sugar |
| | juice of 3 oranges |
| | oranges zest to taste |
| | Grand Marnier |
| | brandy |
| 2 | Tbsp. butter |

Melt butter in pan and add sugar until carmelized. Add juice of oranges and zest. Flame with Grand Marnier and brandy. Add butter, place crepes individually in pan. Fold in half and then in triangles.

*Makes 12 crepes, serves 4*

# The Broiler Room

~~~~~~~~~~~~~~~~~~~~~~~~~~~~~~~~~~~

**THE BROILER ROOM**
Caesar's Tahoe
Highway 50 at Stateline (P.O. Box 5800)
Stateline, NV 89449
(702) 588-3515
Hours: 6:00 p.m. - 11:00 p.m. Friday through Tuesday
Credit Cards: All major
Prices: Moderate
Reservations: Suggested
Specialties: Steak and seafood

*The Broiler Room is known for its prime beef and succulent seafood. It offers a rustic yet elegant atmosphere for fine dining. Traditional dining selections include San Francisco style cioppino, broiled white sea bass, lobster, mixed grill and lamb chops. The Broiler Room has just added a taste of New Orleans to its offerings with Cajun selections prepared in the style of K. Paul's Louisiana Kitchen. The Broiler Room is along the Promenade at Caesar's, next to Cafe Roma.*

# Cioppino

| | |
|---|---|
| 1 | large onion, chopped |
| 1 | medium green pepper, chopped |
| 1 1/2 | c. celery, sliced |
| 1 | carrot, pared and shredded |
| 3 | cloves garlic, minced |
| 3 | Tbsp. olive oil |
| 2 | 1-lb. cans tomatoes |
| 1 | 8-oz. can tomato paste |
| 1 | tsp. basil, crumbled |
| 1 | bay leaf |
| 1 | tsp. salt |
| 1/4 | tsp. pepper |
| 1 | lb. fresh or frozen swordfish or halibut steak |
| 1 | dozen mussels or clams in shell |
| 1 1/2 | c. dry white wine |
| 1/2 | lb. shrimp |
| 1 | lb. scallops |
| 2 | Tbsp. parsley, minced |

Saute onion, green pepper, celery, carrot and garlic in olive oil until soft. Stir in tomatoes, tomato paste, basil, bay leaf, salt and pepper. Heat to boiling, reduce heat, cover, simmer 2 hours. While sauce simmers, clean fish and clams. Stir in wine, add fish, simmer 10 minutes. Add clams, shrimp and scallops. Cover and steam 10 minutes or until done. Ladle into soup bowls and sprinkle with parsley. Serve with sourdough bread or crusty French bread.

*Serves 4*

# Cobb Salad Tossed Tableside

| | |
|---|---|
| 2 | c. iceberg lettuce |
| 1/2 | c. crisp bacon, crumbled |
| 1/2 | c. ham, cubed |
| 1/2 | c. chicken, cubed |
| 1/2 | c. avocado, cubed |
| 1/2 | c. tomato, cubed |
| 1/2 | c. bleu cheese, crumbled |
| 1/2 | c. Jack cheese, cubed |
| 2 | hard boiled eggs, sliced or quartered |
| 1/4 | c. parsley, finely chopped |
| 1/2 | c. red onion, diced |
| 1/2 | c. salad dressing |

Arrange all ingredients, but dressing, in a bowl. Toss with salad dressing.

*Serves 2*

# Bronzed Swordfish

| | |
|---|---|
| 1 | 6-oz. portion swordfish |
| 3 | Tbsp. K. Paul's Seasoning Mix |
| | clarified butter |

Coat both sides of fish with seasoning mix and cook in clarified butter in cast-iron pan until done. (just lightly bronzed).

*Serves 1*

# Pompano Blackened, Acadian

| | |
|---|---|
| 1 | 8-oz. fillet of pompano, 1/2" to 3/4" thick, skinned |
| 2 | Tbsp. butter |
| 1 | Tbsp. lemon juice |
| 1 1/2 | Tbsp. cayenne pepper |
| 1 | Tbsp. salt |
| 1 | tsp. black pepper |
| 1 | Tbsp. thyme |
| 1/2 | red bell pepper, julienned |
| 1/2 | green bell pepper, julienned |
| 1/2 | red onion, julienned |
| 1 | Tbsp. garlic, minced |

In a saucepan, saute pompano in butter.  Combine lemon juice, cayenne pepper, salt, black pepper and thyme and add to the pompano.  Add  bell peppers and onion and saute quickly.  Add garlic and serve at once.

*Serves 1*

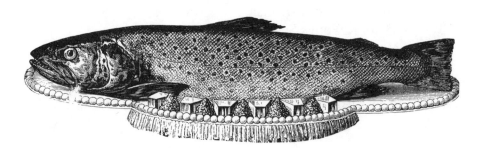

## CAFE ROMA

Caesar's Tahoe Casino

Highway 50 at Stateline (P.O. Box 5800)

Stateline, NV  89449

(702) 588-3515

Hours:  Twenty-four hours a day, seven days a week

Credit Cards:  All major

Prices:  Moderate

Reservations:  None

Specialties:  Varied

*The Cafe Roma, with a restful cafe setting of natural rock and wood, provides an informal meal any time of the day or night.  The extensive menu offers the most popular All-American, South of the Border and Italian favorites for breakfast, lunch or dinner, plus daily specials, all served twenty-four hours a day.  Breakfasts are a treat with a variety of fluffy omelettes and old-fashioned hot and cold sandwiches, spectacular deli-style offerings, Mexican dishes, potato skins with various toppings and sensational salads.  Dinner selections offer even more specialties from the chef - fried chicken, fish and chips and New York steak.  Cafe Roma also features an array of light meals from the Caesar's Spa Fitness Menu.*

# Brochette of Beef

| | |
|---|---|
| 8 | oz. beef, cut in 4 pieces |
| 1 1/2 | oz. onion, diced in large pieces |
| 2 | oz. green pepper, diced in large pieces |
| 3 | oz. cherry tomatoes |
| 5 | oz. rice |
| 3 | oz. brown sauce (see glossary) |

Place meat, onion, pepper and tomato alternately on long skewers. Broil until meat is of desired doneness. Serve on bed of rice covered with brown gravy.

*Serves 1*

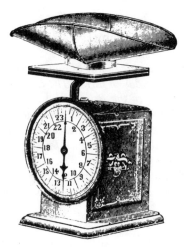

# Pork Verde

| | |
|---|---|
| 8 | lbs. pork shoulder, cubed |
| 1 1/2 | c. flour |
| 3 | Tbsp. salt |
| 2 | Tbsp. black pepper |
| 1/4 | c. oil |
| 3 | onions, chopped |
| 3 | bell peppers, chopped |
| 2 | Tbsp. garlic powder |
| 2 | bunches cilantro, chopped |
| 3 | jalapenos, chopped |
| 2 | c. tomatillos |
| 1 | small can diced green chilies |
| 4 | Tbsp. cumin |
| 2 | Tbsp. ginger |
| 1 | c. sherry |
| 12 | c. chicken |
| 12 | c. beef stock |
| | sour cream |
| 3 | 6" tortillas |

Mix pork with flour, salt and pepper. In a large stock pot brown pork in hot oil. Add onions, bell peppers and garlic powder. Saute 5 minutes. Add cilantro, jalapenos, tomatillos, chilies, cumin, ginger, sherry and stock. Cook 1 1/2 to 2 hours over low heat. Ladle into casserole and spoon sour cream on top. Serve tortillas on the side.

*Makes 1 1/2 gallons*

CAPTAIN JON'S
7220 North Lake Blvd.(P. O. Box 236)
Tahoe Vista, CA 95719
(916) 546-4819
Hours: 6:00 p.m. - 9:30 p.m.
Credit Cards: Visa, Mastercard, American Express
Prices: Moderate to Expensive
Reservations: requested
Specialties: Seafood

*Captain Jon's, one of the fine dining pleasures of the Tahoe scene, is a restaurant where you latch onto something wonderful the first time your are there and can barely bring yourself to try anything else on succeeding visits. You remember that first exquisite dish and want it again. But be brave, try new dishes, they are all outstanding.*

*As with many Tahoe buildings, Captain Jon's could tell some wild tales - from its bordello days, its casino period, from when it was a ferry stop and a post office. These days it is simply one of the best places on the lake to dine, thanks to chef Gino. With its boathouse bar, right on the pier, and its tie-up facilities for boats, Captain Jon's is also one of the greatest places on Lake Tahoe to watch the sun set. Luncheons on the deck, sinful desserts, cocktails in the lounge with taste-tempting hors d'oeuvres, service fit for kings and spectacular views of Lake Tahoe provide a dining experience you will remember and return to.*

45

# Mussels

| 48 | mussels, cleaned and de-bearded |
| 1/2 | c. white wine |
| 1 | tsp. shallots, minced |
| 1/4 | tsp. garlic, minced or pureed |
| 1 | Tbsp. butter |
| 1 | c. cream |
| 1 | Tbsp. parsley, chopped |
| 1/8 | tsp. rosemary |
| | pinch nutmeg |

Steam mussels with wine, shallots and garlic in covered pan until opened. Remove mussels from pan, add remaining ingredients and reduce until sauce lightly coats a spoon.

*Serves 4*

# Escargots Grape

| 24 | snails, rinsed |
| 1 | c. garlic butter (recipe follows) |
| 1/2 | c. dry vermouth |
| 2 | Tbsp. cream |
| 32 | Thompson seedless grapes |

Saute snails in half of garlic butter and the vermouth. Add remaining garlic butter, cream and grapes. Reduce over high heat and serve with French bread.

*Serves 4*

# Garlic Butter

| | |
|---|---|
| 1 | c. butter |
| 1 | Tbsp. garlic pureed |
| 1 | tsp. shallot puree |
| 2 | Tbsp. white wine |
| 1 | Tbsp. parsley, chopped |
| 1/2 | tsp. tarragon |
| | pinch each salt, pepper and cayenne |

Mix above ingredients together.

*Yield 1 cup*

# Duck - Oyster

1      whole duckling, roasted
*Sauce*
1/2  c. duck stock
1/2  c. demi-glace (see glossary)
1      shot brandy or cognac
1/2   c. cream
1/4   tsp. garlic, minced
1/4   tsp. shallots, minced
1      jar Pacific oysters

Roast duck. In a saute pan make sauce by combining stock, demi-glace, brandy or cognac, cream, garlic and shallots and oysters. Reduce. Carve duck, serve with sauce.

*Serves 4*

# Chocolate Mousse

6      eggs, separated
1/2   c. dark, sweet chocolate, melted
1      shot rum
1      shot Grand Marnier
2      c. cream
3      Tbsp. sugar

Whip egg yolks until 3 times volume. Whip whites until stiff. Add melted chocolate and alcohols to yolks, fold in egg whites. Whip cream and sugar together. Top mousse with whipped cream. Chill and spoon into parfait glasses.

*Serves 8*

# *Chez Bernard*

**CHEZ BERNARD**
432 E. 4th St.
Reno, NV 89512
(702) 323-6262
Hours: 5:00 p.m. until closing - Lounge
6:00 p.m. until closing - Dinner, closed Tuesday
Credit Cards: American Express, Visa, Mastercard
Prices: Moderate
Reservations: Suggested
Specialties: French Continental

*Bernard Rault, owner of Chez Bernard, has been in the restaurant business for over thirty-five years. He grew up in Paris and learned the art of a successful restaurateur from his parents. Esconced in Reno now for the past six years, Bernard has attracted a devoted clientele who are known to him by name and who return for his authentic French food and the cozy, intimate, family-style French restaurant atmosphere. It is a very relaxed restaurant, very French-neighborhood type, even though Bernard does tableside cooking. Everything is cooked to order. If you want fettucine, call Bernard a day ahead of time and he will prepare it especially for you. Chez Bernard is famous for its French Onion Soup, and it is particularly good.*

# Baked French Onion Soup

| | |
|---|---|
| 2 | medium onions, sliced |
| 1/4 | lb. butter |
| 1 | Tbsp. flour |
| 1/2 | c. sherry wine |
| 1/2 | c. burgandy wine |
| 1 | qt. water |
| 1 | tsp. caramel color |
| 12 | croutons |
| 4 | slices Swiss cheese |
| 1 | Tbsp. Parmesan cheese |

Saute onions in melted butter until golden brown. Add flour and thicken over low heat. Add wines and cook. When onions are soft and tender, add water and boil. Mix in caramel color. Place finished soup into crocks and add croutons and cheeses. Bake until browned.

*Serves 4*

# Shrimp Normande

| | |
|---|---|
| 24 | jumbo shrimp |
| 1/8 | lb. butter |
| 1 | c. sauterne wine |
| 1/4 | clove garlic, pureed |
| 1 | shallot, minced |
| 1/2 | lb. fresh mushrooms, sliced |
| 1/8 | yellow onion, diced |
| 4 | sprigs parsley, finely chopped |
| | salt and pepper to taste |
| 1 | c. half and half |
| 1/2 | tomato, cubed |

Saute shrimp in butter and wine, along with the garlic and shallots, on low heat until partly done. Add mushrooms, onions and seasonings and simmer for 3 to 4 minutes. Add half and half and tomatoes and reduce. Serve on a bed of rice pilaf.

*Serves 4*

# Caramel Custard

| | |
|---|---|
| 1/2 | c. sugar |
| | water |
| 2 | c. milk |
| 3 | eggs |
| 1/2 | tsp. vanilla |

In sauce pan crystalize sugar on low heat, adding a drop of water and whipping until smooth.  Place this in individual cups.  Mix other ingredients, then pour into cups.  Place cups in shallow pan with water and bake for 45 minutes hour at 375° F.  Serve chilled.

*Serves 4*

# CHINESE FLOWER DRUM

**CHINESE FLOWER DRUM RESTAURANT**
120 Country Club Drive #24 (P.O. Box 6643)
Incline Village, NV   89450
(702) 831-7734
Hours:  11 a.m. - 11 p.m.
Credit Cards: Mastercard, Visa, American Express
Prices:  Moderate
Reservations:  Suggested
Specialties:  Mandarin

*Tucked away in the Country Club Mall in Incline Village, across from the Hyatt Lake Tahoe, is the Chinese Flower Drum, featuring a delicious menu of Mandarin cuisine.  On the menu are many house favorites and seafood dishes with a true Mandarin flair.  Combination dinners are popular choices, with soup, appetizers and a choice of entrees.  The recipes included in this edition, made with dried Chinese mushrooms and lily buds, with hoisin sauce and rice vinegar, indicate the authenticity of Flower Drum.  The service is attentive and pleasant.*

# Hot and Sour Soup

| | |
|---|---|
| 3 | dried Chinese mushrooms* |
| 3 | c. chicken stock |
| 4 | lily buds* |
| 1/8 | c. bamboo shoots |
| 1/2 | c. tofu |
| 1/4 | c. pork, shredded |
| 1 | egg |
| | white pepper |
| | dash of salt |
| 1 | Tbsp. vinegar |
| 1 | Tbsp. cornstarch |
| 1 | Tbsp. water |
| 1 | green onion, minced |

Soak mushrooms for 1/2 hour, until soft, discard stem. Dice. In a stock pot heat to a boil the stock, mushrooms, lily buds, bamboo shoots, tofu and pork. Add egg and stir quickly for about 1 minute. Add pepper, salt and vinegar. Thicken with cornstarch and water blended together. Add green onions and serve immediately.

*Available in Oriental markets

*Serves 3*

# Chicken Salad

| | |
|---|---|
| 3 | chicken breasts |
| 1 | tsp. hoisin* |
| 1 | tsp. hot bean paste* |
| 1/2 | tsp. rice vinegar* |
| 1 | tsp. soy sauce |
| 1 | tsp. sugar |
| 1 | tsp. cooking sherry |
| 1 | green onion, cut in 1" pieces |
| | shredded lettuce |
| 10 | pieces cashew nuts |

Boil chicken until tender. Cool in cold water, then shred the meat. Blend the next 7 ingredients together. Add chicken and mix together. Place on a bed of shredded lettuce. Garnish with cashew nuts.

*Available in Oriental markets

*Serves 3*

# Kung Pao Squid

| | |
|---|---|
| 1 1/2 | lb. fresh squid |
| 2 | tsp. dry red pepper, chopped |
| 2 | Tbsp. sesame oil |
| 3 | cloves garlic, chopped |
| 1 | tsp. cornstarch |

*Sauce:*

| | |
|---|---|
| 1 | Tbsp. sesame oil |
| 1/2 | tsp. salt |
| 2 | tsp. sugar |
| 1 | Tbsp. soy sauce |

Wash and remove membrane from squid. Score deeply lengthwise and crosswise, then cut into rectangles. Combine sauce ingredients and set aside. Stir-fry dried red pepper in oil until peppers turn dark. Add garlic. cornstarch and squid. Stir-fry quickly over high heat until the squid curls up. Pour the sauce onto the squid, boil and serve.

*Serves 4*

# Eggplant with Hot Garlic Sauce

| | |
|---|---|
| 1 1/2 | lb. eggplant |
| 1 | Tbsp. sesame oil |

*Sauce:*

| | |
|---|---|
| 1 | tsp. cooking sherry |
| 1/4 | tsp. salt |
| 1/2 | tsp. MSG (optional) |
| 1/2 | tsp. cornstarch |
| 1 | Tbsp. sugar |
| 1 | Tbsp. soy sauce |
| 1 1/2 | Tbsp. vinegar |
| 2 | Tbsp. water |

*Seasoning:*

| | |
|---|---|
| 1 | Tbsp. chili sauce |
| 1 | Tbsp. garlic, chopped |
| 2 | Tbsp. scallions, chopped |
| 1 | Tbsp. ginger, chopped |
| 3 | Tbsp. oil |

Peel eggplant and cut into 2" x 1/2" thick strips. In a wok stir fry eggplant in sesame oil until soft. Drain the eggplant on paper towels to absorb the grease. Mix sauce in a bowl. Set aside. Mix Seasoning and stir-fry seasoning, add sauce, then eggplant, bring to a boil and serve.

*Serves 4*

# *Cicero's*

**CICERO'S**
1695 So. Virginia St.
Reno, NV 89502
(702) 329-2581
Hours: 11:30 a.m. - 2:30 p.m. Lunch daily
5:30 p.m. - 10:30 p.m. Dinner daily
7:00 p.m. - 2:30 a.m. Live entertainment,
Friday, Saturday
Closed Saturday and Sunday for lunch,
Sunday nights in winter
Credit Cards: American Express, Visa, Mastercard, Diner's Club
Prices: Moderate to expensive
Reservations: Recommended
Specialties: Veal, Fresh Fish, Tableside Cooking

*Cicero's is a new name for an old tradition. The restaurant that housed Reno's famous Vario's is now Cicero's, with the same decor - leaded glass room partitions and chandeliers that have been there for forty years - the same subdued elegance with the friendly overtones of familiar, well-trained waiters. It is a wonderful place to dine if you're in the mood for great pampering, mouth-watering creations and a leisurely, beautifully-served meal. Chef Steve Gessner has a creative mind and uses it to your benefit - for example, prawns and papaya, sauteed - who would have thought? And you will enjoy the repartee that comes along with part-owner Jay Morrison's preparation of one of the best Caesar salads you'll find in the world. Dress up and dine well at Cicero's, then wander into the lounge and listen to jazz, pop, reggae - just about anything that sounds good and is danceable. A great night spot.*

# Prawns Savoy Appetizer

| | |
|---|---|
| 2 | oz. clarified butter (see glossary) |
| 18 | prawns, peeled and deveined |
| 1 | Tbsp. fresh garlic, chopped |
| | salt and pepper |
| 2 | oz. roux (see glossary) |
| 4 | oz. sherry wine |
| 2 | Tbsp. dry mustard |
| 2 | Tbsp. chives, chopped |
| 1 | c. whipping cream |
| 4 | Tbsp. butter |

Heat saute pan with clarified butter and saute prawns lightly until firm.  Add garlic, salt,  pepper, and roux.  Add sherry and flame to clear alcohol.  Stir and allow to thicken.  Add dry mustard, chives and slowly add the cream. Thicken.   Stir butter in slowly. Do not boil.

*Serves 6*

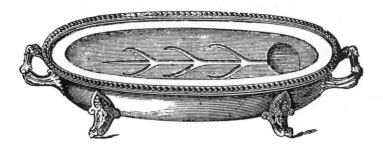

# Black Mussels Fra Diablo

3       oz. olive oil
48      fresh black mussels, well scrubbed and bearded
2       Tbsp. garlic, chopped
        salt and pepper
4       oz. white wine
1/2     c. fresh parsley, chopped
1       tsp. red chilies
        juice of 2 lemons
16      oz. marinara sauce

In a heavy skillet heat olive oil and add mussels, shaking vigorous-ly until open. Add garlic, salt, pepper, wine, parsley, red chilies, lemon juice and marinara sauce. Simmer 8 to 10 minutes. Serve as is for an appetizer or over fresh linguine as a main course.

*Serves 6 to 8*

# Button Mushroom Soup

2     lbs. small white mushrooms, whole
1     small onion, minced
      clarified butter (see glossary)
4     oz. roux (see glossary)
4     oz. sherry wine
16    oz. chicken stock, chicken base, or water
      black pepper to taste
3     Tbsp. dry tarragon
16    oz. heavy whipping cream

Saute mushrooms and onion in clarified butter until soft. Add roux, sherry, and slowly add stock. Allow to thicken. Add pepper and tarragon. Slowly add cream to finish, allowing to thicken enough to keep mushrooms in suspension.

*Serves 6 to 8*

# Rollantini of Chicken

6     8-oz. chicken breasts, boneless, skinless, pounded flat
6     pieces prosciutto ham, thinly sliced
18    leaves fresh spinach
12    slices Swiss cheese
      flour
      egg wash (see glossary)
      clarified butter (see glossary)
2     c. brown sauce (see glossary)

### Rollanti of Chicken (cont.)

Lay chicken breasts on flat surface and place 1 slice ham, 3 spinach leaves, 2 slices of Swiss in center. Roll tightly, chill to set. Dip in flour, then egg wash. Place in hot saute pan with clarified butter, open side down, and brown on all sides. Place in 350° F oven 20 to 25 minutes. Remove from pan, cut off ends and slice breasts into 4 equal pieces. Place heated brown sauce on plate and add 4 pieces of chicken to the sauce.

*Serves 6*

# Scallopine of Veal Forrestere

| | |
|---|---|
| 2 | lbs. veal scallopine, sliced |
| | flour, seasoned |
| | clarified butter (see glossary) |
| 1 | tsp. fresh garlic, chopped |
| 1 | tsp. shallots, chopped |
| | salt and pepper |
| 6 | oz. port wine |
| 1 | lb. white mushrooms, sliced |
| 8 | oz. oyster mushrooms |
| 8 | oz. straw mushrooms |
| 8 | oz. brown sauce (see glossary) |

Lightly dust veal slices in seasoned flour. Saute to a light brown in clarified butter. Add garlic, shallots, salt and pepper. Increase heat and add port wine. Burn alcohol off. Add mushrooms and brown sauce. Cook until thickened slightly. Serve with spaghettini tossed in garlic butter, salt and pepper and fresh parsley.

*Serves 6 to 8*

# Steak & Lobster House

**CRYSTAL BAY STEAK & LOBSTER HOUSE**
Crystal Bay Club/Casino (P. O. Box 37)
Crystal Bay, NV  89402
(702) 831-0512
Hours: 6:00 p.m. - 9:30 p.m. Sunday through Thursday
6:00 p.m. - 10:00 p.m. Friday and Saturday
Credit Cards:  Visa, Mastercard, American Express
Prices:  Moderate
Reservations: Suggested
Specialties:  Steak and Lobster

*Nestled in a far corner of Stateline's Crystal Bay Club, the Steak & Lobster House (a favorite of North Shore locals) draws its clientele back for memorable evenings. Just a few steps out of the casino, it is an oasis of comfortable high-backed, burgundy-colored velour booths, mirrored walls, Renoir and Monet prints, and fresh flowers on beautifully appointed tables.*

*The waiters are quick to refill a coffee cup and pour the wine.  And the tableside service - the presentation of many dishes right at the table - is one of the best shows in town.  The wide variety of specialties makes dinner choices difficult, whether you're the traditional prime rib of beef diner or the Lobster Cardinal type.  Daily specials include chicken, fish or veal.  Seafood and lamb entrees are also offered. Enjoy the North Shore's gem of fine dining.*

# Lobster Cardinal

| | |
|---|---|
| 2 | oz. clarified butter (see glossary) |
| 1 | oz. diced onion |
| 2 | oz. mushrooms,sliced |
| 1/2 | tsp. fresh garlic, chopped |
| 1 | 8-oz. lobster tail, cut into 1/2" cubes |
| 1 | oz. Benedictine |
| 1 1/2 | oz. heavy cream |
| 1/2 | oz. Hollandaise Sauce |
| 1/2 | tsp. fresh parsley, chopped |

Heat saute pan and add clarified butter. Add onion, mushrooms and garlic. Saute until tender. Add lobster and cook until lobster is halfway done. Add Benedictine and flame, then reduce heat until alcohol burns off. Add heavy cream. Reduce until the sauce thickens. Remove from heat and add Hollandaise Sauce. Serve in a casserole and sprinkle with parsley.

*Serves 1*

# Baked Halibut Beurre Blanc

| | |
|---|---|
| 1 | 8-oz. piece halibut steak |
| | salt and pepper to taste |
| 1/4 | oz. lemon juice |
| 1 | tsp. Worcestershire Sauce |
| 1 | oz. flour |
| 1 | oz. clarified butter (see glossary) |
| 2 | oz. white wine |
| 1/2 | oz. lemon juice |
| 1 | bouquet garni (see glossary) |
| 2 | oz. heavy cream |
| 3 | oz. unsalted butter |
| | capers |
| | parsley |

Season halibut with salt and pepper, lemon juice and Worcester-shire Sauce. Dredge in flour and saute on both sides lightly in clarified butter. Place in oven. For the sauce: In pan combine wine, lemon juice and bouquet garni. Reduce on low heat until almost dry, without scorching. Remove bouquet garni. Add heavy cream, again reduce until almost dry. Then add butter, a little at a time, whisking into a smooth sauce. Place halibut on plate. Ladle sauce over top, garnish with capers and parsley.

*Serves 1*

# Poulet Saute Provencale

| | |
|---|---|
| 1 | 8-oz. boned breast of chicken |
| 2 | oz. clarified butter (see glossary) |
| 1 | oz. mushrooms, quartered |
| 1 | tsp. whole thyme |
| 1/2 | oz. onion, diced fine |
| 1/4 | tsp. garlic, minced |
| 1/4 | c. white wine |
| 1 | small whole tomato, peeled and diced |
| 1/8 | c. sliced green olives |
| | parsley |

Saute chicken in clarified butter, remove from pan. Bake in oven until just cooked. Add mushrooms, whole thyme, onion and garlic to pan. Saute together, add wine and reduce. Add tomato. Place chicken on serving plate. Pour sauce over and garnish with green olives and parsley.

*Serves 1*

# Bananas Foster

| | |
|---|---|
| 4 | oz. unsalted butter |
| 1/3 | c. granulated sugar |
| 2 | ripe bananas |
| 1/2 | cup orange juice |
| 1-1/2 | oz. Creme de Banana Liqueur |
| 1-1/2 | oz. rum |
| 1/4 | tsp. cinnamon |
| | vanilla ice cream |
| | whipped cream |
| | toasted, chopped almonds |

Melt butter in pan, add sugar and stir until almost carmelized. Add bananas and continue stirring until bananas soften. Add orange juice and Creme de Banana. Reduce to half. Remove pan from flame, add rum and flambe. As it is flambeing, sprinkle cinnamon over sauce. Serve over vanilla ice cream. Add fresh whipped cream and garnish with toasted almonds.

*Serves 2.*

# The Dory's Oar

Established 1975

**THE DORY'S OAR**

**1041 Fremont Avenue (P. O. Box AH)**

**South Lake Tahoe, CA 95705**

**(916) 541-6603**

**Hours: 11:00 a.m. - 2:00 p.m. Lunch, Monday - Friday**

**5:00 p.m. - 10:00 p.m. Dinner, 7 days a week**

**Credit Cards: Visa, Mastercard, American Express,**

**Diner's Club**

**Prices: Moderate**

**Reservations: None**

**Specialties: Seafood and Live Maine Lobster**

*A self-proclaimed New England-style restaurant, Dory's Oar in South Lake Tahoe is just that, plus a whole lot more. Guests are invited to choose their own live Maine lobster right from the tank while enjoying Dory's seafaring atmosphere. The dining room is decorated with a New England flair - crisp blue and white ruffled curtains are tied back at the windows and pictures of seascapes adorn the walls above the cozy tables. Lunch and dinner fare is served, featuring peel-and-eat-shrimp, baskets of deep-fried clams, oysters or shrimp, seafood quiche and more. From what Dory's calls the "Kansas Coast," there is a selection of premium beef cuts - filet, Porterhouse and the New York, if you'd prefer a meat'n potatoes meal. In the winter, Dory's offers all-you-can-eat crab legs on Tuesday night, plus a number of delicious hot drinks for apres-ski.*

71

# Shrimp Salad

2 1/2   lbs. bay shrimp
1         c. Miracle Whip salad dressing
4         green onions, chopped
3         stalks celery, chopped
1/2      tsp. Tabasco
          juice of 1/4 lemon
          salt and pepper to taste

Rinse and drain shrimp.  Add salad dressing, onions and celery.
Mix well, add the rest of the ingredients.  Mix and chill.

*Serves 10*

# Jumbo Shrimp Cooked in Spiced Beer

1         qt. beer
4         cloves garlic
1         tsp. crab boil
1         Tbsp. parsley
12        large shrimp, 16-20 per pound
4         oz. butter
2         tsp. garlic puree

In sauce pan, combine beer and spices, bring to a boil.  Add
shrimp and cook until shrimp are pink (about 7 minutes).

Serve with drawn butter and garlic puree.

*Serves 2*

# "Murray's" Shrimp

| | |
|---|---|
| 2 | c. beer |
| 2 | c. olive oil |
| 1 | lb. butter |
| 1 | tsp. paprika |
| 3 | tsp. cracked pepper |
| 3 | tsp. Creole seasoning or seasoned salt |
| 1/2 | tsp. crab or shrimp boil |
| 3-5 | cloves garlic, crushed |
| 1 | tsp. cayenne |
| 2 | lbs. large shrimp, in shell |

Combine all ingredients except shrimp over medium-low heat, stirring frequently. Bring almost to a boil then let simmer 15 minutes (keep stirring). When all ingredients are completely blended, add shrimp and cook until done (15-20 minutes). Do not peel shrimp. Serve with hot sourdough bread - dip bread in sauce.

*Serves 6*

# Barbecue Scallops

| | |
|---|---|
| 2 | Tbsp. lemon juice |
| 1 | tsp. salt |
| 1/4 | tsp. black pepper |
| 8 | Tbsp. butter, melted and cooled |
| 1 | lb. medium scallops |
| 8 | slices bacon |
| 1 | lemon, quartered |

Combine lemon juice, salt, pepper and butter in small bowl. Mix well. Toss scallops in butter mixture. Thread scallops and bacon onto a skewer weaving bacon over and under scallops. Brush with remaining butter mixture. Place on barbecue for 4-5 minutes, turning and basting. Serve on heated platters with lemon wedges.

*Serves 2*

# Seafood Quiche

| | |
|---|---|
| 10 | eggs |
| 1 | c. heavy cream |
| | salt and pepper to taste |
| 1 | bunch green onions, chopped |
| 4 | oz. chilled crabmeat |
| 4 | oz. salad shrimp |
| 1 | c. mozzarella cheese, grated |
| 1 | c. Swiss cheese, grated |
| 1 | 10-inch pie crust |

## Seafood Quiche (Cont.)

Beat eggs, add cream, salt and pepper. Add onions, crabmeat and shrimp. Mix in both cheeses and pour into crust. Bake at 375 degrees until firm (about 40 minutes). Let set for 10 minutes before cutting.

*Serves 6-8*

# Char-Broiled Swordfish Steak

2  12-oz. swordfish loin steaks
   salad oil as needed
   maitre d' hotel butter (recipe follows)

Brush swordfish with salad oil, place on char-broiler. Constantly brush swordfish with maitre d' hotel butter while cooking (about 7 minutes on each side).

*Serves 2*

# Maitre d' Hotel Butter

5  oz. butter
   salt to taste
   white pepper to taste
1  tsp. fresh parsley, chopped
1  tsp. lemon juice

Soften butter. Add salt, pepper, and parsley. Stir in lemon juice and heat slowly. (Can be refrigerated for later use.)

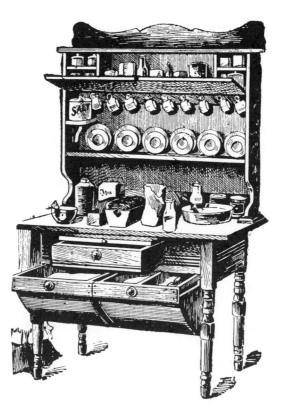

# Eagles' Nest Inn

**EAGLES' NEST INN**
**472 Needle Peak Rd. (P.O. Box 5250)**
**Stateline, NV  89449**
**(702) 588-6492**
**Hours:  7:00 a.m. - 11:00 a.m.  Breakfast**
**11:30 a.m. - 2:30 p.m.  Lunch**
**5:00 p.m. - 10:30 p.m.  Dinner**
**8:00 a.m. - 2:30 p.m.  Sunday brunch**
**Credit Cards:  Visa, Mastercard, Diner's Club**
**Prices:  Moderate**
**Reservations:  Suggested**
**Specialties:  Northern Italian and Continental Cuisine**

*The Eagles' Nest is aptly named, for it sits atop the Sierra Nevada Mountains, commanding views of such breathtaking quality it is difficult to do anything but gaze off into the distance. However, while you're doing that, it's also possible to eat, and at Eagles' Nest the food is high on the list of owner Tito Pordon's quality services for his treasured guests. In the European-style dining room, meals of one kind or another are served all day long. The dishes are unusually good, the ingredients of the highest calibre. The Eagles' Nest is one of the true high spots of Tahoe dining . . . no pun intended.*

# Shrimp Scampi Flambe

| | |
|---|---|
| 5 | shrimp |
| 1 | Tbsp. clarified butter (see glossary) |
| | salt and pepper to taste |
| 2 | oz. garlic, chopped |
| 1 | oz. sherry |
| 1/4 | oz. Poupon mustard |
| 1 | oz. mushrooms, sliced |
| 1 | oz. butter |

In a hot sauce pan, saute shrimp in clarified butter butter, for 1 minute on each side. Add salt, pepper and garlic. Add sherry to stop the cooking process. Add mustard and mushrooms and cook for 1 minute more. Add butter and stire to a creamy consistency.

*Serves 1*

# Steven's Stuffed Chicken Breast

| | |
|---|---|
| 1/2 | lb. cream cheese |
| 3 | c. wild rice, cooked |
| 1 | pippin apple, diced |
| 1 | Tbsp. raisins, optional |
| 1 | Tbsp. walnuts, optional |
| | salt and pepper to taste |
| 8 | spinach leaves |
| 10 | oz. chicken breasts, remove skin and cut into 8 pieces, |
| 1 | oz. butter |
| 1 | Tbsp. shallots |
| 1/2 | c. white wine |
| 1/2 | c. heavy cream |
| 1 | Tbsp. butter |

Blend together cream cheese, rice, apple, raisins, walnuts, salt and pepper and form into golf-ball-size balls. Wrap each in a fresh spinach leaf. Pound the chicken with a mallet to an even thickness. Roll stuffing into the chicken pieces and seal the chicken thoroughly around the mixture. In a sauce pan heat butter and saute chicken until golden brown. Remove chicken and in the same pan, cook shallots, add wine. Add cream. Reduce to a creamy consistency. Add butter. Pour over stuffed chicken.

*Serves 4*

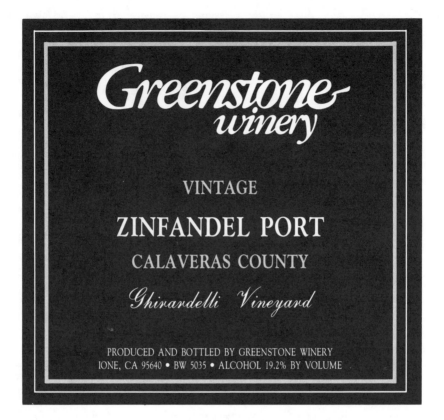

**Character of the wine:** A dessert wine made of 100% Zinfandel grapes that are grown in a Ghiradelli family vineyard that is over 90 years old. The few grapes which are produced are exceptionally complex and rich and produce a unique port.

**Food pairing:** This award-winning wine is the absolutly perfect accompaniment to a rich New York-style cheesecake.

**EL TORO BRAVO**
**10186 Donner Pass Rd. (P.O. Box 2941)**
**Truckee, CA   95734**
**(916) 587-3557**
**Hours:  11:00 a.m. - 10:00 p.m. Daily**
**Credit Cards:  American Express, Visa, Mastercard**
**Prices:  Inexpensive**
**Reservations:  Not required**
**Specialties:  Tex-Mex and Mexican Seafood**

*The popularity of Tex-Mex is understood once you've eaten Ann Goodman's spicy culinary wonders at El Toro Bravo.  From the tortilla chip dip through the albondigas soup, through the appetizers and the entree - until you get to the soothing and wonderful flan for dessert, in fact - your taste buds will be titillated.  Try the seafood specials if you're interested in wonderful, gourmet Tex-Mex.  But the traditional items are there, too, for the diehards who crave their burritos, tacos, huevos rancheros, chili rellenos, enchiladas and tostados.*

81

# Albondigas Soup

| | |
|---|---|
| 1 | lb. ground beef |
| 1 | egg |
| 1/8 | tsp. salt |
| 1 | qt. cold water |
| 1 | onion, diced |
| 3 | cilantro sprigs |
| 1 | carrot, diced |
| 2 | stalks celery, diced |
| 1/4 | c. raw white rice |

Combine the first 3 ingredients and form into meat balls. Set aside. Place water in a stock pot. Bring to a boil and add onions, cilantro, carrot, celery and rice. Add meat balls and simmer until meat is done.

*Serves 4*

# Ceviche

| | |
|---|---|
| 1 | lb. Red Snapper, cubed |
| 6 | green onions, chopped |
| 3 | tomatoes, chopped |
| 1/2 | bunch cilantro, chopped |
| | juice of 8 lemons |
| 1 | c. clam juice |
| 1/4 | tsp. each, salt and pepper |
| 1/2 | tsp. granulated onion |
| 1/2 | tsp. granulated garlic |

Place all ingredients in a ceramic covered dish. Marinate in refrigerator for at least 1 hour.

# Oysters 4-4-4

1/4     bunch parsley
3       cloves garlic, finely chopped
1/4     lb. butter
12      oysters
        juice of 3 lemons
*Toppings:*
1/2     lb. spinach, cooked and chopped
1/4     lb. chorizo (Mexican sausage)
1/2     lb. Cheddar cheese, grated
1/2     lb. Monterey Jack cheese, grated

Place parsley, garlic and butter in small pan and melt.  Shuck oysters, place on oven-proof plate and pour half of melted mixture over oysters.  Bake at 375° F. for 5 minutes.  Fry chorizo until crumbly.  Top 4 oysters with steamed spinach.  Top 4 oysters with chorizo.  Cover all 12 oysters with the grated cheeses and place back in oven until cheese melts.  Place remaining melted butter mixture in small cup and serve as a dip for the oysters.

*Serves 2*

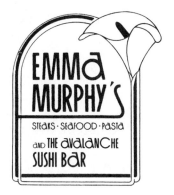

**EMMA MURPHY'S**
425 North Lake Blvd. (P. O. Box 7020)
Tahoe City, CA   95730
(916) 583-6939
Hours:   10 a.m. - 2 p.m Lunch, daily
5 p.m. till closing Dinner, daily
11 a.m. - 3 p.m. Sunday brunch
Credit Cards:  American Express, Visa, Mastercard, Diners Club
Prices:  Moderate
Reservations:  Suggested weekends and holidays
Specialties:  Sushi bar, fresh fish, prime rib

*The good food and excellent service of Emma Murphy's has created a cadre of satisfied customers who return to Emma's whenever they come to Tahoe for their skiing, sunning and relaxing. The sushi bar is on a par with any in the Bay Area, and the general ambience of the restaurant with its Old Tahoe atmosphere is conducive to lingering stays as the sun sets over the startling beauty of Lake Tahoe and its majestic mountains. Live bands perform on weekends.*

# Avalanche Roll

| | |
|---|---|
| 1 | sheet nori (see glossary) |
| 1/2 | c. sushi rice* |
| | Wasabi paste to taste* |
| 1 | med. shrimp coated in tempura and deep fried |
| 1/4 | avocado, sliced |
| 1/8 | English cucumber, peeled, seeded and thinly sliced |
| 1 | tsp. mayonnaise, flavored with a small amount of smelt roe |
| | Garnish with smelt roe* |

On a bamboo roller place a sheet of nori and cover with the rice. Flip over and add a thin strip of Wasabi paste across nori edge closest to you, about the width of an index finger. Lay shrimp, avocado, cucumber and mayonnaise on Wasabi paste. Roll carefully and cover with smelt roe. Slice the sushi into four equal pieces and arrange on a decorative platter. Serve with soy sauce and Wasabi.

*Available in Oriental markets

*Serves 2*

# Empress Court.

**EMPRESS COURT**

Caesar's Tahoe Casino

Highway 50 at Stateline (P.O. Box 5800)

Stateline, NV 89449

(702) 588-3515

Hours: 6:00 p.m. - 11:00 p.m. Friday - Tuesday

Credit Cards: All major

Prices: Moderate to expensive

Reservations: Recommended

Specialties: Szechwan, Cantonese, Mandarin

*The Empress Court features authentic Chinese delicacies from the many regions of China, served in an exotic Far East setting. Specialty drinks include a Rickshaw Delight, Manchu Sting and Passionate Dragon. Complete dinners are offered with appetizers, soup and entrees. An extensive a la carte menu is highlighted by such dishes as Moo Goo Gai Pan, Drums of Heaven, Roast Duck Peking, and the house specialty, Winter Melon Soup. All dinners are served with tea, seasonal fruit and almond fortune cookies. The Empress Court is on Caesar's main casino floor next to Le Posh.*

# Winter Melon Cup with Lotus Seeds

| | |
|---|---|
| 1 | 8-lb. winter melon |
| | chicken stock |
| | salt |
| 1 | oz. dried lotus seeds*, soaked for 1 hour |
| 3 | oz. duck breast meat, finely diced |
| 2 | dried black mushrooms, soaked for 25 minutes, then diced* |
| 3 | oz. lean ham, finely diced |
| 3 | oz. lean pork, finely diced |
| 1 | dried scallop, soaked for 25 minutes, then diced* |
| 1 | Tbsp. rice wine or dry sherry* |
| 2 | slices fresh ginger |
| 1 | egg white, well beaten |
| 1 | Tbsp. cornstarch |
| 1 1/2 | oz. fresh or canned crabmeat |

Select the more attractive end of the melon, wipe it with a damp cloth and scoop out the seeds and the fibrous center. Carve a decorative motif on the skin around the sides and use a sharp knife to make zig-zag cuts around the rim. Fill the melon with boiling stock and add a large pinch of salt. Stand upright in a heatproof dish and place on a rack in a wok or steamer. Cover and steam over briskly boiling water for about 20 minutes. Skin the lotus seeds and use a toothpick to push out the bitter center core. Place the duck meat, mushroom caps, ham, pork, and the scallop in a saucepan, adding the lotus seeds and wine. Ladle the stock from the melon over the ingredients and bring to a boil.

## Winter Melon Cup with Lotus Seeds (Cont.)

.Cook until the lotus seeds are tender, then return this mixture to the melon.  Add the ginger, egg white and cornstarch mixed with a little cold water, and return the melon to the steamer.  Steam for 30-35 minutes, then remove the ginger and stir in the crab-meat just before serving.

*Available in Oriental markets

*Serves 8*

# Chicken Lemon

| | |
|---|---|
| 1 | 2 lb. chicken |
| 2 | Tbsp. light soy sauce |
| 1 | Tbsp. rice wine or dry sherry |
| 2 | Tbsp. lemon juice |
| 1 | c. peanut oil |

*Sauce*

| | |
|---|---|
| 2 | c. chicken stock |
| 3 | green onions, chopped |
| 6 | slices young fresh ginger, shredded |
| 1 | Tbsp. tomato ketchup |
| 3 | Tbsp. lemon juice |
| 1 | Tbsp. sugar |
| 1/2 | tsp. salt |
| 1 | lemon, sliced for garnish |

Clean the chicken and wash well, dry with paper towel and place in a dish. Mix the soy sauce, rice wine or sherry and lemon juice together and rub over the chicken, pouring the remainder inside the cavity. Cover and let stand for 1 hour, turning once, then drain, reserving the marinade. Place chicken on a rack to dry. Heat peanut oil in a wok and fry the chicken over moderate heat on all sides until golden. Transfer to a casserole dish. Pour the reserved marinade over the chicken and add the sauce ingredients. Cover and bring to a boil, simmering very gently for about 1 hour, or until the chicken is tender. Remove the chicken, drain and cut (straight through the bones) into serving portions. Arrange on a plate and place sliced lemon on top. Rapidly boil the sauce until well reduced, then pour the sauce over the chicken and serve.

*Serves 6*

# Sweet and Sour Pork

| | |
|---|---|
| 9 | oz. unsmoked bacon |
| 1/2 | tsp. salt |
| 2 | tsp. rice wine or dry sherry* |
| 1 | egg, well beaten |
| 1 | c. cornstarch |
| | oil for deep-frying |
| 1 | medium green bell pepper, seeds, stems and inner ribs removed, cut into squares |
| 2 | oz. fresh or canned bamboo shoots, thinly sliced |
| 2 | green onions, thinly sliced |
| 3 | cloves garlic, minced |

*Sauce:*

| | |
|---|---|
| 2 | Tbsp. sugar |
| 1 | Tbsp. oil |
| 3 | Tbsp. brown vinegar* |
| 1/2 | c. stock |
| 1 | tsp. cornstarch |
| | salt and pepper |
| 1/2 | tsp. seasame oil* |

Use a sharp knife to closely crosshatch the bacon skin, then cut the bacon into cubes, each with a piece of skin attached. Place in a dish with salt, rice wine and egg. Mix well and set aside for a few minutes. Place the cornstarch in a plastic bag, add the bacon and shake vigorously to coat thickly and evenly. Transfer to a colander and shake off the excess. Heat the oil in a wok to the smoking point and deep-fry the bacon for 1 minute, then lower the heat slightly and continue to fry for about 3 minutes, or until well cooked and crisp on the surface.

# Sweet and Sour Pork (Cont.)

Remove and drain well. Drain off the oil, saving it, and wipe out the wok. Return 2 tablespoons of the oil and stir-fry the pepper, bamboo shoots, green onions and garlic for about 1 1/2 minutes. Add the bacon and mix well, remove to a plate. To make the sauce, pour the sugar and oil into the wok and cook until it turns a light caramel color, stirring occasionally. Add the vinegar and the remaining ingredients and bring to a boil, stirring. Return the bacon and vegetables, stir in the sauce until evenly coated, sprinkle on the sesame oil and serve.

*Available in Oriental markets

*Serves 4*

# Skewered Pork Dipped in Malt Sugar

2        Tbsp. soybean oil
1 1/2    Tbsp. light soy sauce
1        Tbsp. dark or mushroom soy sauce*
1        Tbsp. Fen liquor, rice wine or dry sherry*
1        Tbsp. sugar
1/4      tsp. salt
1        tsp. sesame oil*
1        lb. pork leg, cut into strips
3        Tbsp. malt sugar (maltose)
1/2      c. boiling water.

Mix the first 7 ingredients together and place in a dish with the pork. Mix well and marinate for 2 to 3 hours, turning frequently. Thread the strips of pork on a thick metal skewer and suspend them in a pre-heated 400° F. oven, over a drip tray. Roast for 10 minutes. Mix the malt sugar and boiling water together, stirring until the sugar has melted. Remove the pork from the oven and brush liberally with the syrup, then return to the oven to roast for another 5 minutes. Brush again with syrup, roast again very briefly, then remove from the oven and brush with a final coating of syrup. Cut into slices and arrange on a serving plate. Can be served warm or cold.

*Available in Oriental markets

*Serves 4*

# Steamed Flounder

| | |
|---|---|
| 1 | 12-oz. fresh flounder |
| 2 | dried black mushrooms, soaked for 25 minutes* |
| 6 | slices fresh ginger, shredded |
| 2 | oz. lean pork fillet, shredded |
| 2 | green onions, shredded |

*Seasoning*

| | |
|---|---|
| 2 | Tbsp. Superior Stock* |
| 1/2 | tsp. sesame oil* |
| | pinch white pepper |

Clean and scale the fish and slash along the top of the backbone on either side. Place in the center of an oval heatproof dish that will fit inside a wok or steamer. Drain the mushrooms, squeeze out excess water and shred finely. Arrange mushrooms, ginger, pork fillet and the white parts only of the green onions. along the top of the fish, set the dish on a rack in a wok or steamer, cover and cook over gently simmering water for about 15 minutes or until fish is very tender. Bring the stock and the seasoning ingredients to a boil separately. Pour over the fish and serve at once.

*Available in Oriental markets

*Serves 2*

**FIRE SIGN CAFE**
1785 West Lake Blvd. (P.O. Box 7923)
Tahoe City, CA   95730
(916) 583-0871
Hours:  7 a.m. - 3 p.m. Seven days a week
Credit Cards:  Visa, Mastercard
Prices:  Inexpensive to moderate
Reservations:  Not required
Specialties:  Home-cooked food

*Lake Tahoe's West Shore has been the home for nearly a decade for the perennially popular Fire Sign Cafe - popular with locals, first-time tourists, repeat tourists and the famous names in the area - Steve McKinney, Bill Walsh, Arnold Schwarzenegger, when he's around. A few reasons for the popularity are the absolutely excellently prepared omelettes, specialty sandwiches and hot apple-walnut cobbler.*

*The Fire Sign is Old Tahoe and its premise is old-fashioned. The food will knock you off your feet.*

# Poppy Seed Banana Muffins

| | |
|---|---|
| 2 | eggs |
| 1/2 | c. oil |
| 1/2 | c. honey |
| 1/2 | c. milk |
| 2 | ripe bananas |
| 1 | Tbsp. baking powder |
| 1 | c. whole wheat flour |
| 1 | c. whole wheat pastry flour |
| | small pinch salt |
| 3 | Tbsp. poppy seeds |

In a mixing bowl blend together eggs, oil, honey and milk until it is a very smooth consistency. (Note: When measuring the wet ingredients, it's best to measure the oil before the honey. If the oil is put in the measuring cup first the honey will not stick to the cup when added). In a small bowl mash the bananas with a fork and set aside. In a third bowl mix all dry ingredients together except the poppy seeds. Be sure to sift the 2 flours and the baking powder together and make sure all the dry ingredients are mixed well.

Add the dry ingredients to the mixing bowl of wet ingredients and mix thoroughly until it is a very smooth consistency. Stir in bananas and the poppy seeds. Spoon this mixture into a greased muffin tin so that each cup is a little over 2/3 full. Bake at 350° F. for approximately 14 minutes or until the muffins turn slightly brown around the edges. They should feel fairly soft to the touch when removed and stiffen up while cooling.

*Makes 14 muffins*

# Blueberry Muffins

| | |
|---|---|
| 1/2 | c. oil |
| 1/2 | c. honey |
| 2 | eggs |
| 1/2 | c. milk |
| 1 | c. whole wheat flour |
| 1 | c. whole wheat pastry flour |
| 3 | tsp. baking powder |
| 1 | tsp. salt |
| 1 | c. fresh blueberries |

Cream together oil and honey.  Add eggs one at a time, beating well after each egg.  Add milk. Sift together dry ingredients.  Add to wet mixture.  Fold in blueberries.  Grease 12 muffin tins, fill 2/3 full and bake in preheated 350° F. oven for 12-15 minutes.

*Yeilds 12 muffins*

# Baklava

| | |
|---|---|
| 2 | lbs. walnuts |
| 2 | c. sugar |
| 2 | tsp. cinnamon |
| 2 | lb. filo dough |
| 1 1/2 | lbs. butter, melted |

*Syrup:*

| | |
|---|---|
| 2 | c. honey |
| 1 | c. water |
| | juice of 1 lemon |

Grind walnuts. Combine with sugar and cinnamon. Grease 11 x 16 pan with some of the melted butter. Layer pan with 12 sheets of filo, brushing each with melted butter. Srinkle with 2 cups of nut mixture. Cover with 5 filo sheets, brushing each with melted butter. Sprinkle 2 more cups of nut mixture and cover with 12 filo sheets, brushing each layer with butter. Chill before cutting. Cut pastry into small diamond shapes. Bake in slow oven 300° F. for 1 1/2 hours until lightly browned. Remove from oven. Combine honey, water and lemon juice and cook on medium until the consistency is syrupy. Cool. Pour syrup over hot pastry.

*Yields 75 pieces*

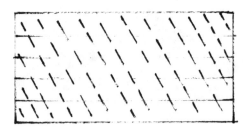

**FRIDAY'S STATION STEAK HOUSE**
Harrah's Lake Tahoe
Highway 50 at Stateline Road (P. O. Box 8)
Stateline, NV 89449
(702) 588-6611
Hours: 11:00 a.m. - 3:00 p.m. Lunch
5:30 p.m. - 11:00 p.m. Dinner
Open seven days a week
Credit Cards: All major credit cards accepted
Prices: Moderate
Reservations: Suggested
Specialties: Steak and Seafood

*Harrah's Tahoe is famous for elegant dining in any of its fine restaurants, and Friday's Station is no exception. Specializing in steaks as well as seafood, delicious sandwiches and several house favorites, Friday's Station is the perfect spot for a business lunch or intimate dinner. Decorated in turn-of-the-century style with crystal leaded glass dividers, oak finish and old-fashioned chandeliers, this popular dining place is not to be missed.*

# Ramekin of Crab and Artichoke

| | |
|---|---|
| 6 | oz. Chenin Blanc |
| 4 | oz. Kirschwasser |
| 8 | oz. Gruyere cheese, grated |
| 8 | oz. Swiss cheese, grated |
| 2 | Tbsp. flour |
| | pinch of nutmeg |
| | pinch of white pepper |
| 2 | Tbsp. unsalted butter |
| 1 | Tbsp. garlic, minced |
| 3 | c. artichoke hearts, quartered |
| 12 | oz. Dungeness crab |
| 3 | Tbsp. Parmesan cheese, grated |

For the sauce, flambe wine and Kirschwasser. Toss Gruyere and Swiss cheese with flour. Stir cheese mixture into wine until smooth. Season with nutmeg and white pepper. Melt butter in another saute pan, add garlic, artichoke hearts and crab. Toss until hot. Add cheese sauce and portion into 3 ounce ramekins. Top with Parmesan cheese and place under broiler until cheese is melted. Serve immediately.

*Serves 4*

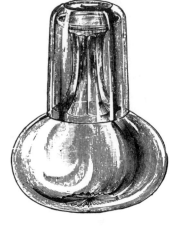

# Galena Forest Inn

**GALENA FOREST INN**
17025 Mount Rose Highway
Reno, NV 89511
(702) 849-2100
Hours: 5:00 p.m. until closing, Wednesday through Sunday
Credit Cards: Visa, Mastercard
Prices: Moderate
Reservations: Required
Specialties: Swiss Cuisine

*Set at the edge of the Galena Forest on the scenic Mount Rose Highway leading from Reno to Lake Tahoe, Galena Forest Inn specializes in authentic Swiss cuisine - in a big way. The abundant portions satisfy the most sophisticated palate and the hungriest of skiers. Just minutes from Reno and a breathtaking short drive from the ski areas of the eastern slope of the Sierra, the restaurant is easily accessible and worth the trip.*

# Oysters Rockefeller

|         | Rock salt                    |
|---------|------------------------------|
| 1       | c. shallots, chopped         |
| 1/2     | c. parsley, chopped          |
| 1 1/2   | c. spinach, chopped          |
| 1/2     | c. flour                     |
| 1       | c. melted butter             |
| 1       | c. oyster water              |
| 1       | clove garlic, minced         |
| 1/2     | tsp. salt                    |
| 1/4     | tsp. cayenne                 |
| 1/4     | c. anchovies, minced         |
| 4       | oz. Pernod                   |
| 3       | dozen fresh oysters.         |

Fill a pie pan with rock salt for each serving. Place in oven to preheat salt. While salt is heating, make sauce by putting shallots, parsley and spinach through food processor. Stir flour into melted butter and cook 5 minutes. Do not brown. Blend in oyster water, garlic, salt and cayenne. Stir in processed greens and anchovies. Simmer covered for 20 minutes. Remove cover, stir in Pernod and cook until thickened. Place half-shells (6 per serving) on hot rock salt. Fill each shell with an oyster. Put sauce in a pastry bag and dispense enough to cover each oyster. Bake in preheated 400° F. oven for about 5 minutes or until edges of oysters begin to curl.

*Serves 6*

# Spetzli

| | |
|---|---|
| 1 | lb. flour |
| 6 | eggs |
| 1/2 | oz. salt |
| 2 | oz. oil |
| 1 | pinch nutmeg |
| 1 | pt. lukewarm water |

Place flour in a bowl. In a second bowl, combine remaining ingredients, then add to the flour and quickly knead the mixture until it blisters. Pass dough through a colander into salted boiling water. Remove spetzli as they rise to the surface and cool them immediately in cold water. Finish by sauteing them in butter.

*Serves 10*

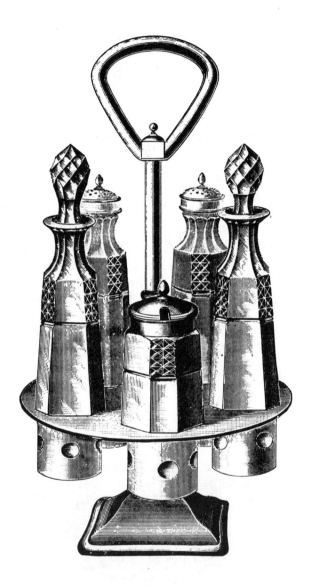

**HEISS'**
**107 E. Telegraph**
**Reno, NV 89701**
**(702) 882-9102**
**Hours: 4:30 p.m. - 10:00 p.m. Sunday through Thursday**
**4:30 p.m. - 11:00 p.m. Friday and Saturday**
**Credit Cards: American Express, Visa, Mastercard**
**Prices: Moderate**
**Reservations: Suggested on weekends and parties over six**
**Specialties: Steak, Lobster**

*Just a block south of the Carson City Nugget Casino, half a block off the main drag, sits one of the best restaurant in the capitol city, Heiss'. It's been there, serving statesmen and politicians, for nearly two decades, and with new owner, Ross Miller, the Heiss' tradition is carried on, serving the best cuts of meat and wonderful seafood dishes. The seafood casserole is delectable and the appetizer mushrooms are great with a drink at the bar if you're not hungry enough for one of those big steaks. Heiss' is quiet, intimate, with a piano bar, a loyal following - and is one of the best-kept secrets in the Carson Valley.*

# Gourmet Sauteed Mushrooms

| | |
|---|---|
| 2 | oz. clarified butter (see glossary) |
| 5 | large mushroom caps |
| 1 | clove fresh garlic, minced |
| | lemon pepper |
| | salt or Knorr Swiss Seasoning |
| 2 | oz. cocktail sherry |
| 1 | oz. chicken broth |
| | grated Parmesan cheese |

In a saute pan heat butter, add mushroom caps and saute at high heat until light brown. Turn caps, add garlic, sprinkle with seasonings. Add cocktail sherry. (Pan should be hot enough to flame the sherry - watch your eyebrows!) Add chicken broth and simmer for about 3 minutes. Sprinkle with grated Parmesan cheese.

*Serves 1*

# Potato and Cheddar Soup

| | |
|---|---|
| 6 | medium potatoes, peeled and diced |
| 6 | chicken broth |
| 3 | bay leaves |
| 2 | medium carrots, diced |
| 1 | small bunch green onions, diced |
| 1 | tsp. salt |
| 1/2 | tsp. white pepper |
| 1/2 | tsp. granulated garlic |
| 1/2 | oz. maggi seasoning |
| 1/2 | lb. sharp Cheddar cheese, grated |
| 1/2 | c. sour cream |

Cover potatoes with chicken broth and bring to a boil. Add bay leaves. Cook until potatoes are tender. Using a wire whisk, mash potatoes as much as possible (finished product should be smooth with a few lumps of potato). Add carrots, green onions, and seasonings. Simmer for 1/2 hour. Add grated cheese, mix with wire whisk until dissolved. Add sour cream and stir until smooth. (Note: This soup will not break down like a cream soup and can be kept hot for long periods of time.)

*Yields 2 quarts*

# Daytona Shrimp Stuffing

| | |
|---|---|
| 1 | c. onions, diced small |
| 1 | c. green bell peppers, diced small |
| 1 | c. celery, diced small |
| 4 | Tbsp. butter or margarine |
| | pinch of salt |
| | pinch of white pepper |
| 1/2 | Tbsp. dry mustard |
| 5 | drops Tabasco Sauce |
| 1/4 | c. flour |
| 1 | c. milk or cream, heated |
| 5 | oz. bay shrimp |
| 1/4 | c. dry sherry |
| 1/2 | lb. bread cubes |
| 12 | Ritz crackers, crushed |

Saute onions, green peppers and celery in butter until tender. Add seasonings. Add flour and stir for 3 minutes. Stir in hot milk. Add shrimp and sherry. Transfer to mixing bowl and mix in bread and crushed Ritz crackers. (Consistency should be like moist turkey stuffing.) This stuffing can be used with any seafood, for example: Roll a ball of shrimp stuffing inside flounder or sole fillets and bake; or press 1 ounce of stuffing on butterfly shrimp and bake.

*Yields approximately 5 cups*

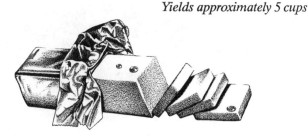

**HUGO'S ROTISSERIE**
**Hyatt Lake Tahoe**
**Lakeshore Boulevard and Country Club Drive (P.O. Box 3239)**
**Incline Village, NV  89450**
**(702) 831-1111**
**Hours:  6:00 p.m. - 10:00 p.m.  Sunday through Friday**
**6:00 p.m. - 11:00 p.m.  Saturday**
**Credit Cards:  All major**
**Prices:  Moderate to expensive**
**Reservations:  Recommended**
**Specialties:  Continental, featuring five duckling dishes**

*The only restaurant located on the Incline shore of Lake Tahoe, Hugo's offers daz-
zling sunset views while you're attempting to make your selections from a varied
fine dining menu. The Hugo's staff is known for its friendliness, the salad bar and
dessert bar have been known to entice diners back for seconds, and the duckling
dishes are really superb. Nicely decorated, with a wealth of greenery and a tiered
arrangement of tables which allows everyone a view of the lake, Hugo's offers a
lovely, romantic evening.*

# Deep Fried Calamari with Gribiche Sauce

2       6-oz. calamari steaks
2       c. flour
2       eggs, beaten
2       c. fresh bread crumbs
        frying oil

Cut calamari steaks into 1/2" strips.  Coat with flour and dip into eggs.  Coat with bread crumbs.  Drop into deep fryer with oil at 350° F. until golden brown.  (Do not overcook as calamari will become tough.)  Serve with Gribiche Sauce.  (recipe follows)

*Serves 2*

# Gribiche Sauce

1       hard-boiled egg, chopped
1/2     c. white wine vinegar
1/2     pint salad oil
1/2     c. mayonnaise
1       Tbsp. capers, chopped
1       dill pickle, chopped
1/2     Tbsp. Worcestershire Sauce
        salt and pepper
        lemon wedge

Combine all ingredients and blend thoroughly.  Serve with calamari strips.  Reserve leftover sauce for hot or cold roast beef.

*Makes 1 1/2 cups*

# Hugo's Duckling with Orange Sauce

1        duck
*Marinade:*
1        Tbsp. sherry wine
1        Tbsp. orange juice
1        tsp. salt
1/2      tsp. orange zest
1/2      tsp. lemon zest
         pinch ground cloves
1        bay leaf, crushed
1/2      cinnamon stick
1        quart salad oil
1/2      c. sesame oil
1/2      Tbsp. oregano
1        Tbsp. sweet basil
1/2      Tbsp. thyme
1        Tbsp. rosemary, crushed
1/4      Tbsp. sage
1/2      c. anise seeds
1        Tbsp. fennel seeds
1        Tbsp. paprika

Combine first 8 ingredients and bring to a quick boil. Remove
and add the remaining 10 ingredients. Mix together thoroughly.
Cover the duck with the mixture and marinate for 4 to 5 hours.
Remove the duck from the marinade and drain off excess. Place
duck in a roasting pan and cook in oven for approximately 1 1/2
hours at 350° F.

*Serves 2*

# Orange Sauce

| | |
|---|---|
| 1 | c. sugar |
| 1 | quart duck or chicken stock |
| 1/4 | c. cider vinegar |
| 1/2 | c. orange juice |
| 1/2 | tsp. ground cloves |
| 1/2 | tsp. fennel seeds |
| 1/2 | tsp. anise |
| 1 | c. butter |
| 1/2 | c. flour |
| 1 | Tbsp. each orange and lemon zest poached in white wine |
| | salt and pepper |
| 1 | Tbsp. orange liqueur or Grand Marnier |

Carmelize sugar but do not burn. Add duck or chicken stock, cider vinegar, orange juice, cloves, fennel and anise and simmer for 30 minutes. Thicken stock with butter and flour (roux, see glossary) and cook another 30 minutes. Then strain the sauce through a fine sieve. Add orange and lemon zest to sauce. Correct taste with salt and white pepper. Add liqueur. Serve the sauce with the duck.

*Makes 1 quart*

# Veal Medallions

| | |
|---|---|
| 14 | dried morels |
| 1 | oz. butter |
| 4 | 3-oz. veal medallions |
| 2 | shallots, chopped |
| 1 | oz. brandy |
| 1 | pt. heavy cream |
| 2 | oz. lobster meat, cooked |
| | salt and pepper |

Soak the morels in 1 cup of warm water for a 1/2 hour. Heat half of the butter and saute the veal medallions. When finished, remove the veal and keep warm. Using the same pan add the shallots and flame the brandy. Pour in the morel soaking liquid and reduce by 2/3. Add the heavy cream and reduce until you have a good consistency. Add the cooked lobster meat and the morels. Blend in the remaining butter and season with salt and pepper. Pour the sauce over the medallions.

*Serves 2*

ON THE LAKE

**JAKE'S ON THE LAKE**
780 North Lake Blvd. in the Boatworks Mall (P. O. Box 6925)
Tahoe City, CA  95730
(916) 583-0188
Hours:    4:30 p.m. - 1:l5 a.m. Bar
5:30 p.m. - 10.:30 p.m., Sunday-Thursday, Dinners
5:30 p.m. - 11:00 p.m., Friday and Saturday, Dinners
Credit Cards:  Visa, Mastercard, American Express
Prices:  Moderate
Reservations:  Suggested
Specialties:  Seafood

*If you're looking for the "in" spot near the water in Tahoe City, don't miss Jake's
on the Lake, a local favorite for years. Specializing in seafood dishes such as Trout
Amandine, Scallops Maison and Scampi, Jake's also offers the fresh catch of the
day and a full seafood bar featuring fifteen items for snacking, including Clams
Casino, Clams Rockefeller and calamari. Richly decorated, using exquisite wood
accents, glass and plants, there is a cascading waterfall at the bar and a beautiful
view of the lake from windows overlooking Tahoe City's private marina. The restaurant also features a full wine list on the back of the menu, as well as the owner's
private reserve wine list, not to be overlooked. For those who prefer other than
seafood, Jake's offerings include steaks, Chicken Tarragon and rack of lamb, along
with cheeseburgers, chicken sandwiches and fresh salads.*

# Clams Casino

| | |
|---|---|
| 6 | lbs. fresh clams (10 per pound) |
| 1 | lb. softened butter |
| 1/4 | c. half and half |
| 1/2 | tsp. garlic puree |
| 2 | Tbsp. Rose's lime juice |
| 2 | Tbsp. catsup |
| 1 | tsp. Worcestershire Sauce |
| 1/4 | c. scallions, chopped |
| 1/2 | tsp. ground white pepper |
| 1 | small can diced pimentos |
| 1/2 | c. bacon bits |
| | grated Parmesan cheese |
| | bread crumbs |

Clean and shuck the clams, discard half of the shell and loosen clam meat from shell. Cream butter with all but last two ingredients. Spread clam with generous amount of butter mixture and sprinkle with cheese and bread crumbs. Place under broiler until butter sizzles and bread crumbs brown. Be careful, the shells get very hot!

*Serves 6 (10 each)*

116

# Au Poivre (Peppercorn Sauce)

| | |
|---|---|
| 2 | c. demi-glace (see glossary) |
| 1 3/4 | Tbsp. freshly ground black pepper |
| 1/2 | Tbsp. Dijon mustard |
| 1/2 | Tbsp. sour cream |
| 1 | dash Tabasco |
| 1/2 | Tbsp. whole green peppercorns |
| 1 | Tbsp. brandy |
| 1 | dash Worcestershire Sauce |

Simmer all ingredients together, add more pepper to taste. Serve over red meat or poultry.

*Makes 2 cups*

# Hula Pie

1      box Nabisco Famous Wafers
3      oz. melted butter
1/2    gallon macadamia nut ice cream
       heavy, dark chocolate fudge topping
       diced macadamia nuts
       whipped cream

Grind wafers to the consistency of ground coffee. Blend in butter. Press firmly onto the bottom of a 9" straight-edge cake pan. Freeze until hard. Soften ice cream until you can mold it with a spatula or large "putty knife." Fill cake pan evenly, molding an even dome of ice cream. Freeze 4 hours or until very hard. Spread with dark fudge topping (use hot water to smooth it) as thick as you like. Freeze for 1 hour, unmold, cut with hot, wet knife and garnish with nuts and whipped cream.

*Serves 8-12*

# Josephine's
## PASTA & PIZZA CO.

**JOSEPHINE'S**
Commercial Row (P. O. Box 58)
Truckee, CA 95734
(916) 587-9291
Hours: 5:00 p.m. - 10:30 p.m. Daily
Credit Cards: Mastercard, Visa
Prices: Inexpensive to Moderate
Reservations: Not required
Specialties: Italian veal & chicken

*Located on historic Commercial Row in Truckee, Josephine's has one of the largest selections of imported and domestic beers from which to choose, as well as great Italian food. Knotty cedar booths are accented by an antique brick wall, ceiling fans, and interesting food pictures adorn the walls. Josephine's famous pasta dishes are made fresh daily, including the special "ravioli of the week" creation. The authentic surroundings at this rustic Truckee spot include strands of garlic bulbs, old-fashioned pasta-making tools and lattice work. The service is attentive and personal - this is a great place for the entire family's evening of casual dining.*

# Pasta Josephine's

| | |
|---|---|
| 4 | 6-oz. boneless chicken breasts |
| 4 | oz. green bell pepper, sliced |
| 4 | oz. red bell pepper, sliced |
| 4 | oz. onion, sliced |
| 1 | Tbsp. oil |
| 1 | Tbsp. butter |
| 2 | c. cream |
| 1 | Tbsp. basil |
| 1 | Tbsp. oregano |
| 1/2 | c. Parmesan cheese (reserve a little for garnish) |
| 24 | oz. cooked fettucine |

Saute chicken, bell peppers and onion in oil and butter. Add cream, herbs and cheese and reduce. Toss with cooked fettucine. Garnish with freshly grated Parmesan cheese.

*Serves 4*

# Fettucine Carbonara

| | |
|---|---|
| 1 | tsp. garlic, finely chopped |
| 40 | snow peas |
| 1 | Tbsp. butter |
| 2 | c. cream |
| 1 | c. Parmesan cheese, freshly grated (reserve a little for garnish |
| 6 | oz. thinly sliced prosciutto |
| 24 | oz. cooked fettucine |

### Fettucine Carbonara (Cont.)

Saute garlic and snow peas in butter. Add cream, simmer. Add cheese and prosciutto. Reduce until thickened. Toss with cooked fettucine. Garnish with parmesan cheese.

*Serves 4*

# Amaretto Torte

| | |
|---|---|
| 1/2 | lb. butter |
| 1/2 | c. sugar |
| 6 | egg. yolks |
| 1/2 | c. flour |
| 7 | Amaretto cookies, ground |
| 1 | c. miniature chocolate chips |
| 6 | egg whites |

Beat butter and sugar until pale in color. Add egg yolks and beat until creamy. Add flour, ground cookies and chocolate chips. Beat egg whites until stiff and fold into batter. Pour into 9 inch cake pan that has been buttered and floured. Bake for 30 minutes at 350° F.

*Serves 12*

**LAKE TAHOE DINNER CRUISES**
Ski Run Marina  (P.O. Box  14292)
South Lake Tahoe, CA   95702
(916) 541-3364
Hours:  Buffet available on ski shuttles
Buffet available on daytime cruises
Dinner available on evening dinner-dance cruises
Credit Cards:  American Express, Visa, Mastercard,
on night-time and ski shuttle cruises only
Prices:  Moderate
Reservations:  Required
Specialties:  Prime Rib and Halibut

*The Tahoe Queen is a must when visiting Tahoe, and for a romantic evening, whether you're tourist or resident, a dinner-dance aboard this sternwheeler is a wonderful and exciting experience.  The splendid scenery of the Tahoe Basin from the middle of the lake - the snow-capped mountains, the pines and firs marching up the mountainsides, the unparalleled blue of the sky and the lake - plus the excellent beef and fish, make a dinner cruise a treat you'll remember forever.  Apres ski parties are a bonus evening in the wintertime, and the ski shuttles to Squaw Valley, Alpine Meadows and Northstar from South Shore are the easy way to get to opposite-shore ski destinations.  Day cruises in the summer to Emerald Bay give a historic overview of Tahoe times.*

# Tahoe Twister

| | |
|---|---|
| 2 | oz. rum |
| | orange juice |
| | 7-up |
| | Mai Tai mix (pineapple/citrus base) |
| 1 | fresh orange slice |
| 1 | fresh pineapple spear |

In a 12-oz. glass, mix rum with equal parts orange juice, 7-up and Mai Tai mix. Serve with a fresh orange slice and a pineapple spear.

*Serves 1*

# Scarlet O'Hara

| | |
|---|---|
| 2 | oz. rum |
| | dash of orange bitters |
| | strawberry daiquiri mix |
| 1 | fresh strawberry |

In blender mix rum, bitters and daiquiri mix.  Pour into 12-oz. glass and add fresh strawberry.

*Serves 1*

# Sierra Snowball

| | |
|---|---|
| 2 | oz. rum |
| | splash white creme de menthe |
| | pina colada mix |
| 1 | fresh pineapple spear |

In blender mix rum, creme de menthe, pina colada mix and top with fresh pineapple spear.

*Serves 1*

# Tahoe Steamer

| | |
|---|---|
| 2 | oz. tuaca |
| 1/8 | tsp. cinnamon |
| | apple cider, heated |
| | whipped cream |

1cinnamon stick

To tuaca add cinnamon and stir in hot apple cider to fill a 12-oz. glass. Top with whipped cream and insert cinnamon stick.

*Serves 1*

# Smuggler's Snuggler

2       oz. peppermint schnapps
        hot chocolate
        whipped cream
        chocolate shavings
1       Oreo cookie

To peppermint schnapps add hot chocolate to fill a 12-oz. glass. Top with whipped cream, sprinkle with chocolate flakes and serve with a Oreo cookie.

*Serves 1*

# Loud Louie

1 1/2   oz. brandy
1 1/2   oz. Kahlua
        coffee
        whipped cream
        splash of green creme de menthe

To brandy and Kahlua add coffee to fill a 12-oz. glass. Top with whipped green and pour creme de menthe over the top.

*Serves 1*

**LANZA'S**

7739 North Lake Blvd. (P.O. Box 1016)

Kings Beach, CA   95719

(916) 546-2434

Hours:  5:00 p.m. - 10:00 p.m. Sunday - Thursday

5:00 p.m. - 10:30 p.m. Friday and Saturday

Credit Cards:  Mastercard and Visa

Prices:  Inexpensive

Reservations:  Not required

Specialties:  Italian

*For years Jerry and Joe Lanza, mother and son, have run this popular Italian restaurant. With tables decorated in traditional red-checkered tablecloths, Lanza's is a nostalgic sight. Also, the front end of the Cadillac that seems to barge through the barroom wall will bring back a few wistful moments to some of you. Each night Lanza's serves up a different specialty, but you can always get your favorite Italiano dinners. If you've never tried lumaconi, do so at Lanza's. It is shells stuffed with beef, cheese and spinach and baked. Mama mia!*

# Lanza's Special Spumoni

| | | |
|---|---|---|
| 1 | pt. | raspberry sherbet |
| 1 | pt. vanilla ice cream | |
| 1 | pt. | chocolate ice cream |
| 2 | pts. heavy whipping cream | |
| 2 | c. roasted almonds, sliced and crushed | |
| 1 | can dark red cherries, or fresh cherries | |
| 1 | pt. pistachio ice cream | |

Use a tube-type mold and on the inside (smallest) circumference, thinly layer the sherbet (let sherbert and ice cream stand at room temperature for about 20 minutes to soften.) On the outside (widest) circumference, layer the vanilla ice cream. On the bottom, layer the chocolate ice cream. Refrigerate. Whip the cream. Add almonds to the cream and blend. Spoon whipping cream mixture into hollow left around the mold. Dot cherries around the top of the whipping cream, then push down into the bottom of the mold. Refrigerate. Cover the top layer of the mold with pistachio ice cream and freeze. To cut, run hot water over the metal of the mold, then unmold and slice.

*Serves 8*

**LA STRADA**
Eldorado Casino
345 No. Virginia Street
Reno, NV 89505
(702) 786-5700
Hours: 5:00 p.m. - 11:00 p.m.
Credit Cards: All major
Prices: Moderate
Reservations: Recommended
Specialties: Northern Italian

*From the sumptuous Italian hors d'ouevres to the soothing taste of gelato, La Strada is a definite treat for Northern Nevadans and their visitors. With decor reminiscent of Old Italy, and beautiful Italian classical background music, an evening at La Strada - Reno casino style - is charming. On the menu are homemade specialties verging on the sinful - ravioli, fettucine and gnocchi - plus the regular veal, chicken and seafood entrees. West coast wines are featured, over 150 of them, with the best values in varietals as well as the highest quality.*

# Fettucine a la Eldorado

| | |
|---|---|
| 1 | lb. fettucine |
|   | olive oil |
| 6 | oz. butter |
| 6 | oz. heavy cream |
| 3 | oz. prosciutto ham, julienned |
| 3 | oz. fresh mushrooms, sliced |
| 3 | oz. frozen peas |
| 1 | egg, beaten |
| 5 | oz. Parmesan cheese |
|   | salt, pepper and nutmeg to taste |

Cook fettucine in boiling salted water until al dente. Drain, coat very lightly with olive oil, set aside. Heat butter in skillet until hot. Add fettucine and heat. Add heavy cream, prosciutto, mushrooms and peas. Simmer for 3 minutes, but do not allow to boil. Add the egg and cheese (the sauce will immediately thicken). Add salt, pepper and nutmeg.

*Serves 4*

# Saute Scampi

| | |
|---|---|
| 16 | prawns |
| 1/2 | c. all-purpose flour |
| 1/8 | lb. butter |
| 1/2 | tsp. garlic, minced |
| 1/2 | tsp. shallots, minced |
| | ground pepper to taste |
| 1/2 | c. white wine |
| 1/2 | c. cream |
| 1/4 | c. bechamel sauce (recipe follows) |
| 1 | tsp. lemon juice |
| 1 | pinch fresh parsley, chopped |
| | fresh sliced mushrooms (optional) |

Peel the shrimp, leaving the final shell section and tail intact. Devein by using a sharp knife to butterfly along the back of the shrimp. Be careful not to cut completely through the shrimp. Remove any vein material by rinsing carefully under cold water. Dust the cleaned shrimp in flour. Heat the butter in a saute pan on medium-low heat. Allow to get hot, but don't burn. Add the shrimp to the heated butter and cook until the shrimp are no longer translucent and are firm. Add the garlic, shallots and pepper to the shrimp and shake pan to mix contents evenly. Add the white wine and reduce (allow to simmer) for 30 seconds. Add the whole cream and the bechamel sauce and allow to reduce an additional 30 seconds. Finally add the lemon juice, the fresh parsley and if desired, the mushrooms.

*Serves 2*

# Bechamel Sauce

1/8      lb. butter
1/2      c. flour
1 1/2    c. whole cream
         pinch of salt and pepper
1        pinch granulated garlic
1/2      c. white wine

Using a sauce pan, melt the butter on medium heat. Add the flour slowly, continually stirring, making a roux. Cook the roux slowly for 5 minutes (don't scorch the flour). Add the cream and stir until the sauce is smooth. Add the salt, pepper, garlic and white wine. Stir and allow to cook 30 minutes on low heat.

# La Table Française

**LA TABLE FRANCAISE**
3065 W. 4th St.
Reno, NV 89503
(702) 323-3200
Hours: 6:30 p.m. - 10:00 p.m. Tuesday - Saturday
Credit Cards: Mastercard, Visa
Prices: Moderate to expensive
Reservations: Required
Specialties: French

*La Table Francaise - tres chic, tres intimate, a place for a rendezvous, an anniversary, a romantic evening. Serving delectable French haute cuisine, La Table Francaise is an event in itself. Tableside cooking is done with a very Gallic flair, and although you may watch closely, the secrets remain with the cook. La Table Francaise will turn into a love affair for you, so be ready for her charms.*

# Soupe au Pistou

| | |
|---|---|
| 1 | lb. string beans, cut in 1" slices |
| 1 | potato, sliced |
| 3 | large tomatoes, peeled and chopped |
| | salt and pepper to taste |
| 2 | qts. chicken broth or beef consomme, heated |
| 1/2 | lb. vermicelli |
| 6 | cloves garlic, mashed |
| 1 | stalk basil, mashed |
| 4 | Tbsp. olive oil |
| 1/4 | c. Parmesan cheese |

Place the string beans into a stockpot with the potato, tomatoes, salt and pepper. Add broth or consomme, bring to a boil and then simmer for 1 hour. Add the vermicelli. Continue to simmer until ready to serve. Pound garlic and basil together. Add olive oil, making a paste and add this to the soup. Ladle into soup bowls. Sprinkle Parmesan cheese on top. Serve immediately.

*Serves 4 to 6*

# Sea Perch Farsi Riviera

| | |
|---|---|
| 2 | lbs. sea perch |
| 2 | egg yolks |
| 8 | oz. butter |
| 1/4 | c. bread crumbs |
| 1 | tsp. chives, finely chopped |
| 1/4 | c. chablis |

## Sea Perch Farsi Riviera (Cont.)

Remove the backbone of the sea perch. Combine egg yolks, butter, bread crumbs and chives and stuff the fish with the mixture. Place the fish in a baking dish and add chablis. Bake at 325° F. for 12 to 15 minutes. Serve at once.

*Serves 2*

# Crepes

| | |
|---|---|
| 3 | eggs |
| | pinch of salt |
| 1/3 | c. sugar |
| 1 1/2 | c. milk |
| 1 | c. flour |
| 2 | Tbsp. butter |

Place eggs, salt and sugar in a food processor, using off-on strokes. Add milk slowly, blending. Add flour. Blend. In a 6" crepe pan melt butter and add to mixture. Pour 2 tablespoons of batter into crepe pan. Tilt pan immediately so that batter will spread over the entire bottom of the pan. Cook on both sides. Wipe pan with cheesecloth after making each crepe.

*Yields batter for 30 crepes*

# Crepes au Curry

| | |
|---|---|
| 1 | tsp. butter |
| 1 | tsp. chopped shallots or Bermuda onions |
| 1/2 | c. chablis |
| 2 | Tbsp. curry powder |
| | salt to taste |
| | pinch of cayenne pepper |
| 1/4 | c. heavy cream |
| 1 | tsp. butter |
| 16 | shrimps, cooked and shelled |
| 1/2 | c. lump crab meat |
| 30 | crepes |

For the sauce, melt butter in sauce pan with shallots or Bermuda onions, let simmer for a few minutes, add chablis. Reduce, add curry, salt and cayenne pepper. Add the heavy cream and let simmer. Keep 1/3 of the sauce on the side. Melt 1 tsp. butter in a saucepan, add the cooked shrimp and crab, saute for 2 minutes, then add curry sauce. (Reserve 2 Tbsp. of the sauce). Stir ingredients together. Place crepes in an open-face position. Put 2 Tbsp. of the shellfish mixture on each crepe. Fold and roll the crepes until they are tubular in shape. Place reserved curry sauce on top of the crepes. Heat crepes in 375° F. oven for 8 to 10 minutes.

*Serves 6 to 8*

# Clafouti aux pommes

6       apples
6       Tbsp. sugar
4       eggs
1       Tbsp. butter

The day before, peel and core the apples. Mash them and
sprinkle with sugar. Refrigerate. The next day beat the eggs and
mix them with the apples. Melt butter in souffle dish and put mixture in. Place in 400° F. oven for 20 minutes to 1/2 hour. Sprinkle
with sugar and serve hot.

*Serves 6*

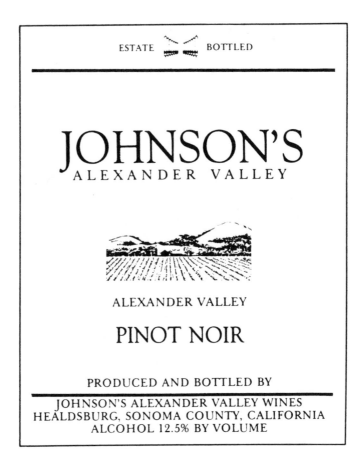

# JOHNSON'S
### ALEXANDER VALLEY

ALEXANDER VALLEY

## PINOT NOIR

PRODUCED AND BOTTLED BY

JOHNSON'S ALEXANDER VALLEY WINES
HEALDSBURG, SONOMA COUNTY, CALIFORNIA
ALCOHOL 12.5% BY VOLUME

A dark red color with a silky texture, this Pinot Noir is excitingly full-bodied. It has a youthful, ripe-cherry aroma and a tantalizing full-fruit flavor with a tinge of herbaceousness.

This wine is excellent with lamb, veal and pork. Also, try it with barbecued turkey.

**LE MOULIN**
**Peppermill Casino**
**2707 So. Virginia St.**
**Reno, NV  89502**
**(702) 826-2121**
**Hours:  6:00 p.m. - 11:00 p.m. Daily.**
**Credit Cards:  All major**
**Prices:  Moderate to expensive**
**Reservations:  Accepted**
**Specialties:  Veal, Fresh Fish, Elk**

*The Peppermill Hotel Casino opened their gourmet restaurant, Le Moulin (meaning the mill), in December of 1986 and added a touch of class to Reno fine dining. Le Moulin features an extensive continental menu with classical French cuisine as well as California nouvelle, and an award-winning wine list.  The chefs' preparation of haute cuisine includes only the finest ingredients - fresh herbs, fresh field fowl, mushrooms hand selected from Washington and Oregon, and the finest meats.  The service is classically French, with many items prepared tableside.  The atmosphere is contemporary but the food and service is the kind steeped in old-fashioned quality.*

# Glazed Red Swiss Chard

1        large bunch red Swiss chard, cleaned and roughly chopped
2        Tbsp. walnut oil
1/2      tsp. caraway seeds
1        Tbsp. orange marmalade
3 1/2    Tbsp. raspberry wine vinegar
1        Tbsp. port wine, mixed with a pinch of cornstarch
         fresh nutmeg
         salt and pepper to taste

Saute the red Swiss chard for a moment in the walnut oil and
caraway seeds. Add the marmalade and vinegar and briefly saute
until all the flavors are well blended (1 to 2 minutes). Add the
port and cornstarch, heat until mixture thickens. Season with nutmeg, salt and pepper to taste.

*Serves 2*

# Crevettes Sauteed a la Verona

1        Tbsp. clarified butter (see glossary)
1        Tbsp. olive oil
5        prawns, cleaned and dredged in flour
1/8      tsp. fine herbs
1/8      tsp. garlic
1        Tbsp. butter
         juice of 1/2 a lemon
1        oz. vermouth

### Crevettes Sauteed a la Verona (Cont.)

Place clarified butter and oil in pan and heat.  Add prawns and saute until done.  Drain off fat and add herbs, garlic, butter and lemon juice.  Saute prawns briefly with vermouth, then place prawns on a bed of linguine.

*Serves 1*

# Stuffed Quail

4       quail
1 1/3   c. wild rice, cooked
6       oz. Camembert cheese
        salt and pepper to taste

Clean the cavity of each quail.  Set aside.  Mix cooked wild rice with Camembert cheese.  Place 1/4 of the mixture into each quail.  Bake at 325° F. for approximately 25 minutes or until done.

*Serves 4*

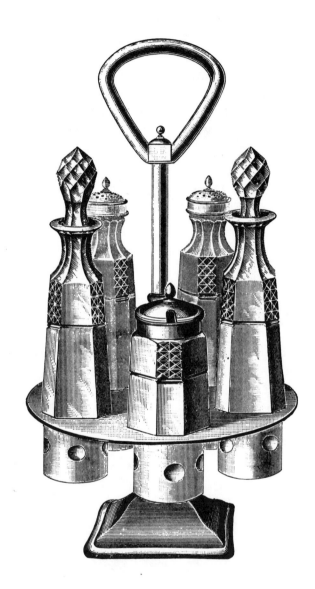

# "Leonardo's"

LEONARDO'S

2450 So. Virginia St.

Reno, NV  89501

(702) 827-6200

Hours:  5:30 p.m. - 11:00 p.m.

Credit Cards:  Mastercard, Visa, American Express

Prices:  Moderate to expensive

Reservations:  Suggested and honored

Specialties:  Northern Italian Cuisine

*Leonardo's has become the in place in Reno for special occasions - and rightly so, for they prepare everything from scratch.  From a very large menu you can order to your heart's delight such items as calamari, Pork Bombay (tenderloin of pork in curry cream with chutney), Pork Madagascar (garlic and wine cream sauce, green and pink peppercorns over pork tenderloins), plus numerous pasta dishes, steaks and chicken entrees.  Leonardo's also makes their own ice cream, Italian fruit pies and cheesecakes.  The service is exceptional, the food worth any celebration.*

# Caesar Salad

|       |                                      |
|-------|--------------------------------------|
|       | juice of 1/2 a lemon                 |
| 3     | anchovy fillets, mashed to a paste   |
| 1/4   | oz. Worcestershire Sauce             |
|       | garlic                               |
| 1     | tsp. Dijon mustard                   |
| 12    | Tbsp. vegetable oil                  |
| 4     | Tbsp. red wine vinegar               |
| 1     | egg, coddled                         |
| 1     | head romaine lettuce                 |
| 3     | Tbsp. Parmesan cheese                |
| 1     | oz. plain croutons                   |
|       | pepper to taste                      |

Combine lemon juice, anchovies, Worcestershire, garlic and mustard in bowl. Add oil, vinegar and coddled egg. Blend together well. Add romaine lettuce, cheese, croutons and pepper. Toss well.

*Serves 2*

# Fettucine Alfredo

|        |                                 |
|--------|---------------------------------|
| 1/2    | oz. butter                      |
|        | touch of fresh garlic           |
| 8      | oz. heavy cream                 |
|        | ground pepper to taste          |
| 4      | oz. Parmesan cheese, grated     |
| 6 - 8  | oz. fettucine noodles           |

### Fettucine Alfredo (Cont.)

Melt butter in pan, add garlic and saute. Add cream and pepper and bring mixture to a boil. Add the Parmesan cheese, stir until smooth. Add noodles, toss and serve.

*Serves 2 as an appetizer, 1 for a main course*

# Steak Diane

| | |
|---|---|
| 1/2 | oz. oil |
| | Dijon mustard |
| 8 | oz. fillet mignon, center cut |
| 1 | oz. butter |
| 1 | oz. shallots, minced |
| 1/2 | oz. garlic |
| | dash Worcestershire Sauce |
| 1 | oz. burgandy |
| 6 | oz. mushrooms, sliced |
| 1 | oz. brandy |
| 4 - 6 | oz. brown sauce (see glossary) |
| 1/2 | oz. heavy cream |

Heat oil in pan. Brush mustard on both sides of meat and cook to desired doneness. Remove from pan. Melt butter in pan, add shallots, garlic, Worcestershire Sauce, burgandy and mushrooms. Saute for a few minutes. Flame with brandy. Add brown sauce and cream. Return meat to pan and heat.

*Serves 1*

# Bananas Foster

| | |
|---|---|
| 3 | Tbsp. brown sugar |
| 2 | oz. creme de banana liqueur |
| 1 | banana, cut in small pieces |
| 1/2 | oz. 150-proof rum |
| | cinnamon and sugar mixture |
| | vanilla ice cream |

Place brown sugar in pan. Add liqueur and stir until smooth. Add bananas and saute until soft. Add rum and ignite. Sprinkle cinnamon and sugar mixture into flame. Stir until flame goes out. Serve bananas over ice cream.

*Serves 2*

**LE POSH**
Caesar's Lake Tahoe
Highway 50 at Stateline (P.O. Box 5800)
Stateline, NV   89449
(702) 588-3515
Hours:  6:00 p.m.  Wednesday - Sunday
Credit Cards:  All major
Prices:  Expensive
Reservations:  Suggested
Specialties:  Nouvelle cuisine

*Le Posh is recognized as one of Northern Nevada's most elegant restaurants. It boasts a wide variety of award-winning nouvelle cuisine specialties - light, not heavy on the sauces - including steamed lobster served with baby vegetables and white wine; salad nouvelle with butterleaf lettuce, asparagus, cashews with a raspberry vinaigrette dressing; Quail Lucullus; and boneless breast of Muscovy Duck in raspberry sauce. Le Posh offers a full selection of domestic and imported wines. A captain, a waiter and a busman serve each table, candlelight flickers and reflects in the etched glass and crystal - you are indeed in a posh place.*

# La Tarte Fine Chaude Aux Pommes Acidulees (Acid Apple Tart)

    puff pastry
6   apples, peeled, cored and sliced thin
    confectioners' sugar

Roll out a layer of puff pastry to 1/8 inch. Round the shape. In a pie plate, arrange the apples 1 on top of the other, cover with puff pastry and confectioners' sugar. Bake in convection oven until the pastry is golden brown.

*Serves 2*

# Les Fraises au Poivre (Old Creole Style Peppered Strawberries)

        egg whites
1       lb. sugar
4 1/2   oz. flour
4 1/2   oz. butter, melted
        vanilla to taste
1/2     c. whipping cream
1       Tbsp. butter
2       Tbsp. cracked black pepper
1       oz. Grand Marnier
24      strawberries
2       Tbsp. sugar
1       oz. Couvoissier cognac

## Les Fraises au Poivre  (Cont.)

Lightly whip egg whites and sugar, then mix in flour, melted butter and vanilla.  Divide in 2 and bake at 375° F. for about 10 minutes.  Place this prepared pastry shell on a plate, cover the bottom of the shell with whipped cream.  In a saucepan, melt 1 Tablespoon of butter, add cracked pepper and Grand Marnier.  Then quickly add strawberries and sugar and flame with the cognac.  Once flamed, served in the pastry shell.

*Serves 2*

**MARDI GRAS**

Eldorado Casino

345 No. Virginia St.

Reno, Nevada   89505

(702) 786-5700

Hours:  Twenty four hours, seven days a week

Credit Cards:  All major

Prices:  Inexpensive to moderate

Reservations:  Not required

Specialties:  Chinese food from 11:00 a.m. - 3:00 p.m.

*Just one of the five outstanding restaurants in the Eldorado Hotel Casino is the Mardi Gras, serving a full menu of breakfast, lunch and dinner items, and a great list of Chinese specialties available for lunch.  The cafe is open all day and all night, with the traditional late night and early morning breakfast fare, such as Belgian waffles, pancakes, a host of pastries and muffins, and of course eggs any way you like them.  The endless menu offers sandwiches, salads, dinner entrees - a dish for every taste or whim.*

# Cashew Chicken

| | |
|---|---|
| 1/4 | c. vegetable oil |
| | pinch of salt |
| 1/2 | lb. chicken breast, thinly sliced |
| 80 | snow peas |
| 1 | stalk celery, thinly sliced |
| 1/2 | onion, diced |
| 1 | 5-oz. can bamboo shoots, diced |
| 1 | 4-oz. can water chestnuts |
| 1 | small can mushrooms, sliced |
| | pinch of sugar |
| 1/2 | c. oyster sauce* |
| 1/4 | c. soy sauce |
| 3/4 | c. chicken stock |
| 2 | Tbsp. cornstarch, diluted in |
| 1/2 | c. water |
| 80 | whole cashew nuts, unsalted |

Heat oil in wok or skillet until very hot. A haze will form over the hot oil, and a droplet of water in the oil will immediately sizzle. Add salt and chicken and cook, stirring constantly for 2 minutes. Add the snow peas, celery, onion, bamboo shoots, water chestnuts, mushrooms and sugar. Stir vigorously for 2 more minutes.

# Cashew Chicken (Cont.)

Add the oyster sauce and soy sauce, stirring for 2 minutes. Add the stock and bring to a fast boil. Add diluted cornstarch while the contents of the wok are boiling. It will thicken quickly. Add the cashews and stir 5 seconds. Remove from heat and serve immediately with steamed white rice.

*Available in Oriental markets

*Serves 4*

**M.S. DIXIE CRUISESHIP**
760 Highway 50 (P.O. Box 1667)
Zephyr Cove, NV  89448
(702) 588-3508
**Hours:  Call for precise times and dates**
**Credit Cards:  American Express, Visa, Mastercard**
**Prices:  Moderate**
**Reservations:  Suggested**
**Specialties:  Steak and Fish**

*The M.S. Dixie Cruiseship,  one of Tahoe's favorite paddle wheelers, offers daily scenic cruises in the summertime, with food and beverage service.  An evening of dining on the Dixie is, however, exciting, refreshing and unusual.  Featuring choices of an 11-ounce New York steak or filet of sole stuffed with shrimp and crab and drenched with Hollandaise, the Dixie menu, simple though it is, offers you the finest quality.   If you can get one of the best dinners on the lake while cruising its aquamarine surface, you will feel yourself indeed in the middle of the "fairest picture the whole earth affords."*

C R U I S I N '   L A K E   T A H O E

# Bleu Cheese Dressing

| | |
|---|---|
| 1 | oz. white vinegar |
| 1 | oz. lemon juice |
| 1 | Tbsp. coarse ground pepper |
| 1/2 | c. onions, dried |
| 1 | c. warm water |
| 2 | c. bleu cheese, crumbled |
| 2 | c. mayonnaise |
| 2 | c. sour cream |

Mix vinegar, lemon juice, pepper and onions with warm water. Let stand for 20 minutes. Add bleu cheese, mayonnaise and sour cream. Blend together and chill before serving.

*Serves 6*

# Thousand Island Dressing

| | |
|---|---|
| 2 | c. mayonnaise |
| 1 | Tbsp. celery salt |
| 1 1/2 | c. sweet pickle relish |
| 1 | oz. simple syrup |
| 1 | c. cocktail or chili sauce |
| 1 | Tbsp. mustard |

Blend ingredients in a large bowl. Refrigerate in an airtight container.

*Serves 6*

OB'S PUB & RESTAURANT
Commercial Row (P. O. Box 1285)
Truckee, CA  95734
(916) 587-4164
Hours:  11:30 a.m. - 10:30 p.m. Daily
Credit Cards:  American Express, Mastercard, Visa
Prices:  Inexpensive to moderate
Reservations:  Not required
Specialties:  Homemade Soups, Fresh Fish, Prime Rib

*OB's Pub & Restaurant is a veritable institution in Truckee, a convivial eatery with simple yet wonderful and varied food, waiters who are as sought after as the dinner specials, and an entertainment schedule that offers something for everyone.*

*Six or seven times throughout the year, OB's creates special evenings, designed to pack the house and keep the customers happy. An annual pre-Christmas fashion show, with Truckee-only goods, is a big attraction, as are the perennial New Year's Eve parties and - of course - the St. Paddy's day bash.*

*For a drink - Watney's on tap, first-class liquor in the well drinks and excellently-chosen wines - or for a full-fledged dinner in the privacy of a wooden booth - OB's is a hands-down winner. A perfect example of old Truckee, the building itself is at least a century old, and artifacts decorating the rustic walls include well-preserved examples of turn-of-the century tools amid the clusters of antique tables and chairs.*

# Guacamole

| | |
|---|---|
| 2 | avocadoes, mashed |
| 1/2 | tomato, diced |
| 1 | Tbsp. lemon juice |
| 1 | Japanese chili pepper, crumbled |
| 1 | clove garlic, pressed |
| | pinch salt, black pepper |

Combine all ingredients well, and serve with chips.

*Serves 4*

# Coquilles Saint Jacques

| | |
|---|---|
| 5 | lbs. scallops |
| 1 | qt. white wine |
| 1 | c. heavy cream |
| 1 | bay leaf |
| 1/2 | c. dry sherry |
| | roux (see glossary) |
| | salt and pepper to taste |
| 1 | lb. button mushrooms |
| 1 | Tbsp. butter |
| 10 | slices of Swiss cheese |
| | paprika |
| | parsley |

## Coquilles Saint-Jacques (Cont.)

Poach scallops in white wine until three-quarters cooked. Strain and reserve half the liquid. Boil reserved liquid, cream, bay leaf and sherry on low heat. Thicken with roux until sauce heavily coats a spoon. Add salt and pepper. Saute mushrooms in butter and add to scallops while sauce simmers for 20 minutes on low heat. Add sauce to scallops and stir gently. Place each portion in an ovenproof dish with a slice of Swiss cheese on top. Sprinkle with paprika, broil until cheese is browned. Sprinkle with chopped parsley and serve.

*Serves 10*

# Raspberry Zinfandel Butter

1       c. raspberry wine vinegar
1       c Zinfandel
4       small shallots, minced
1       clove garlic, minced
2       lbs. soft butter
        parsley

Bring raspberry wine vinegar to boil. Add Zinfandel, shallots and garlic. Let boil until reduced to 1 cup. Cool. Whip together butter and wine mixture until the consistency is smooth. Place in plastic or glass container and refrigerate.

Broil meat or fish. Place 1 ounce portion of butter mixture on top, serve with chopped parsley. Allow butter to melt partially over entree before serving.

*Yields approximately 3 cups*

# Rosemary Chicken

| | |
|---|---|
| 2 | oz. lemon juice |
| 2 | oz. olive oil |
| 6 | cloves garlic, minced |
| 2 | tsp. fresh rosemary, minced |
| 1/4 | tsp. hot red peppers, crushed |
| | salt and pepper to taste |
| 4 | 8-oz. chicken breasts |
| 2 | Tbsp. butter |
| | fresh parsley, chopped |

Combine first 6 ingredients in food processor and mix thoroughly. Quarter chicken breasts and marinate in the lemon mixture at least 8 hours. Saute chicken in butter on medium heat 3 to 4 minutes on each side. Top with chopped parsley and serve.

*Serves 4*

# Banana Nut Bread

*Wet Ingredients:*

| | |
|---|---|
| 2 3/4 | lbs. bananas (weight with peels on) |
| 1/2 | c. honey |
| 3/4 | c. melted butter |
| 1/4 | c. plain sour cream |
| 1/3 | Tbsp. pure vanilla extract |
| 2 | eggs, slightly blended |

*Dry Ingredients:*

| | |
|---|---|
| 1 | c. whole wheat flour |
| 1 | c. all-purpose white flour |
| 1 1/3 | Tbsp. baking soda |
| 1 1/3 | c. walnuts, mashed |

Blend the wet ingredients together. In a separate bowl blend the dry ingredients together. Slowly mix dry ingredients into wet. Mix thoroughly with beaters or whip. Do not overblend or batter will get tough. Make sure dough is well-blended. Bake in 2 loaf pans, equally measured, on middle shelf at 325° F. for 1 1/4 hours.

*Serves 8 to 10*

# Original
# Old Post Office
# Coffee Shop

**OLD POST OFFICE COFFEE SHOP**
**5245 North Lake Blvd, (P.O. Box 331)**
**Carnelian Bay, CA 95711**
**(916) 546-3205**
**Hours: 6:00 a.m. - 3:00 p.m. Breakfast, lunch daily**
**Credit Cards: None**
**Prices: Inexpensive**
**Reservations: Not required**
**Specialties: Breakfast**

*The Original Old Post Office is indeed a former post office - 1936 through 1975 vintage. The service is good and the food is reminiscent of weekends home from college being stuffed with good food by your mom. Norma, who is full of fun and good cheer, is as much a fixture on the North Shore as her restaurant. The Old P.O. is just a neat place to eat. The clientele is regular Old Tahoe, plus returning visitors and a few celebrities stopping by when they're in town. The waffles are the best at the lake, the lunchtime chili is superb.*

# Homemade Maple Syrup

| | |
|---|---|
| 7 | c. water |
| 2 5/8 | lbs. sugar |
| 3 1/8 | lbs. brown sugar |
| 3 | Tbsp. lemon juice |
| 1 1/2 | Tbsp. maple flavoring |

Bring first 4 ingredients just to a boil then add maple flavoring. Store in refrigerator.

*Yields about 7 cups*

# Bread Rolls

| | |
|---|---|
| 4 1/2 | c. warm water |
| 3 | Tbsp. yeast |
| 6 | Tbsp. sugar |
| 8 1/2 | c. flour (or a half cup more or so for right consistency) |
| 3 | Tbsp. salt |
| | salad oil |

Mix water, yeast and sugar. Gradually add flour and salt. Knead. Add salad oil. Cover and let rise. Punch down and let rise again. It will double in size. Punch down. Form rolls. Let rest. Bake when risen at 450° F. until rolls are brown. Reduce to 425° F. and bake 5 to 7 minutes more.

*Makes 2 dozen rolls*

# Thousand Island Dressing

| | |
|---|---|
| 1 | quart mayonnaise |
| 2 1/4 | c. ketchup |
| 1 | Tbsp. Worcestershire Sauce |
| 1/2 | tsp. paprika |
| 1/4 | c. mustard |
| 3/4 | c. relish |

Mix all ingredients and refrigerate indefinitely.

*Makes 7 cups*

# Pancake Batter

| | |
|---|---|
| 1 1/4 | lb. wheat flour |
| 3 1/4 | lb. white flour |
| 10 | oz. sugar |
| 5 | oz. baking powder |
| 2 | tsp. salt |
| 1/4 | tsp. nutmeg |
| 2 | tsp. cinnamon |
| 22 | eggs |
| 1/2 | c. salad oil |
| 1/2 | gallon buttermilk |
| 1 | c. milk |
| 3 1/2 | tsp. vanilla |

Mix dry ingredients. Mix wet ingredients and add to dry. Beat until smooth. Heat skillet and pour on pancake batter. Turn when lightly brown around the edges.

*Serves 25*

Santino

*Eschen Vineyards*
Fiddletown
*Zinfandel*

Alcohol 14.2% by Volume

Produced & Bottled by Santino Wines, Plymouth, Amador County, California

**Full-bodied, with a rich raspberry aroma, this wine adds a peppery snap blended with the flavor of currants. It is pleasing to drink now or is further enhanced with a few years of bottle ageing.**

**Serve this Zinfandel with Amador County leg of lamb. Also excellent when served with chocolate.**

**THE PASSAGE**
Highway 267 and Commercial Row (P.O. Box 2659)
Truckee, CA 95734
(916) 587-7619
Hours: 10 a.m. - 3 p.m. Lunch, summer only
10 a.m. - 3 p.m. Sunday Champagne brunch
5:30 p.m. until closing Dinner, nightly
Credit Cards: Visa, Mastercard, American Express, Diner's Club
Prices: Moderate
Reservations: Recommended
Specialties: International

*It's easy at The Passage to believe yourself to be in a different century, for the past lingers along the sidewalk in front of this century-old building and wafts through the bar and dining room where in the late 1880s the original hotel restaurant occupied these same rooms. The food is imaginative and good, the selections vast. Premium wines are sold by the glass. International dinners include Cajun Shrimp, California Chicken Saltimboca, Basque-style steak. The desserts are also international - and yummy. The service is excellent, the waitresses knowledgeable longtimers who love what they do, and the atmosphere warm, inviting and nostalgic.*

# Pisco Sour

| | |
|---|---|
| 1 1/2 | oz. Pisco |
| 1 1/4 | oz. sweet and sour mix |
| 3/4 | oz. Roses lime juice |
| 1 | Tbsp. sugar |
| 1 | egg white |
| | lime wedge |

Blend all ingredients and garnish with a lime wedge. Serve in a tall, salt-rimmed glass.

*Serves 1*

# Shrimp-Filled Artichoke

| | |
|---|---|
| 4 | artichokes |
| 1 1/3 | c. mayonnaise |
| 1 1/3 | c. grated swiss cheese |
| 1 1/3 | c. bay shrimp or crab |

Steam artichokes. Remove inner leaves, being sure to remove the choke and hairs that are attached to the heart. Remove enough leaves to fill the artichokes with about a cup of filling. Mix together and stuff the artichokes with the filling. Put all filled artichokes in an pan with 1" of water. Cover with foil and heat at 350° F. for 10 minutes, or until they are hot all they way through.

*Serves 4*

# French Loaf Salad

| | |
|---|---|
| 1 | 10-inch round French bread |
| 2 | Tbsp. garlic butter |
| | salad greens |
| 1/4 | c. olive oil |
| | juice of 1 lemon |
| 1 | small jar artichoke hearts |
| 1 | can hearts of palm, sliced |
| 1 | small can shoestring beets |
| 1 | hard-boiled egg |

Slice off top of bread, hollow out to form a bowl, reserving insides for another use. Rub "bowl and lid" with garlic butter. Toss greens with olive oil and lemon juice. Place greens into bread bowl and arrange remaining ingredients on top of salad and set lid on slightly askew.

*Serves 2*

# Fish or Chicken with Orange Butter

| 1/4 | c. butter |
| 1/2 | c. grated orange rind |
| 1 | tsp. orange juice |
| 1 | tsp. tomato paste |
| | salt and pepper |
| 4 | 8-oz. fish fillets or 1 chicken, quartered |

Melt butter and mix well with remaining ingredients.  Baste fish
or chicken while broiling.  Serve any remaining butter on the side
as a dipping sauce.

*Serves 4*

# Normandy- Style Seafood Omelette

*Filling:*

| 1 | medium onion, sliced |
| 1 | clove garlic, minced |
| 1/2 | c. olive oil |
| 1 | large can diced tomatoes or 8 medium tomatoes, skinned, seeded and diced |
| 1 | Tbsp. tomato paste |
| 1 | bay leaf |
| | salt and pepper to taste |
| 1/4 | lb. snapper |
| 1/4 | lb. calamari, cut into rings |
| 1/4 | lb. bay shrimp |

# Normandy-Style Seafood Omelette (Cont.)

*Each Omelette:*

| | |
|---|---|
| 1 | Tbsp. heavy cream |
| 3 | eggs, separated |
| | dash cream of tartar |
| 1 | Tbsp. butter |
| 1/2 | c. mozzarella cheese, grated |

Preheat oven to 350° F. Prepare filling by sauteing onion and garlic in olive oil until onions are soft. Add diced tomatoes, tomato paste, bay leaf, salt and pepper to taste. Bring to a boil, then simmer for 1/2 hour. Add seafood for the last 5 minutes. Be careful not to overcook.

Assemble omelette by adding heavy cream to yolks. Whip until well blended, set aside. Add dash of cream of tartar to whites and whip until peaked. Heat omelette pan with 1 Tbsp. butter. Pour egg yolks into pan, then spread whites evenly over yolks. Cook until the egg yolks are set. Top with 1/4 of the filling and 1/2 cup mozzarella. Bake at 350° F. until the egg whites rise and the cheese is melted to bubbling. Serve open face.

*Serves 4*

# Moussaka

| | |
|---|---|
| 2 | large eggplants |
| 2 | Tbsp. salt |
| 1 | c. all-purpose flour |
| 1 | c. olive oil |
| 1 | lb. bulk sausage meat |
| 2 | c. onion, chopped |
| 2 | lbs. lean ground lamb |
| 1 | tsp. salt |
| 1 | tsp. oregano, dried, crumbled |
| 2 | cloves garlic, minced |
| 1 | c. tomato puree |
| 1/4 | c. fresh parsley, minced |
| | salt and fresh-ground pepper to taste |
| 1 | c. red wine |
| 12-14 | fresh spinach leaves |
| 1/2 | lb. fresh mushrooms, sliced |
| 1 | Tbsp. butter |
| 1/2 | c. all-purpose flour |
| 2 | c. light cream |
| 1/2 | tsp. salt |
| | nutmeg to taste |
| 1/2 | c. ricotta cheese |

Preheat oven to 400° F. Peel and slice eggplants crosswise. Salt and place in a single layer on paper towels for 30 minutes. Pat dry. Place flour in a paper bag and shake a few eggplant slices until coated. Heat oil in a large skillet and lightly saute eggplant slices. Set aside. Brown sausage meat in the skillet. Drain off fat, reserving 2 Tbsp. Set aside. Saute onion in 1 Tbsp. reserved fat, in the skillet, and add to reserved sausage meat.

## Moussaka (Cont.)

Brown lamb in the skillet, seasoning with salt and oregano. Add to reserved sausage mixture. In 1 Tbsp. fat, saute garlic in the same skillet until golden. Add tomato puree, parsley, salt and pepper. Mix well and add wine and reserved meat mixture. Simmer, uncovered, until almost all liquid is absorbed. Butter a 5 quart casserole. Layer eggplant on the bottom. Cover with meat mixture. Add spinach leaves and top with mushrooms. Melt butter in a saucepan until foamy. Sprinkle with flour, cook and stir for 3 minutes. Gradually stir in cream, cook and stir until smooth and thickened. Season with salt and nutmeg and pour over casserole. Top with ricotta cheese. Bake for 1 hour.

*Serves 8*

# Basque Steak

| | |
|---|---|
| 4 | 8-oz. top sirloin steaks |
| 12 | strips bacon, chopped |
| 1 | onion, diced |
| 12 | oysters, shucked |

Charbroil steaks and butterfly them. Meanwhile, saute bacon, add diced onions. Saute until limp, remove from heat and add oysters. Divide mixture on the 4 steaks and fold closed. Serve immediately.

*Serves 4*

# Chilaquiles

| | |
|---|---|
| 1 | 3-lb. chicken |
| 18 | 2-day-old tortillas |
| | oil for deep frying |
| 1 | 10-oz. can Mexican green tomatoes |
| 1 | clove garlic, peeled |
| 1 | onion, finely minced |
| 2 | Tbsp. fat |
| 1 1/4 | c. chicken stock |
| | salt and pepper to taste |
| 1 1/2 | c. sharp Cheddar cheese, loosely packed |
| 1/2 | c. sour cream |
| 1 | c. plus 3 Tbsp. heavy cream |

Cook the chicken in enough salted water to cover for 1 hour. Remove meat from bones and set aside. Preheat oven to 350° F. Cut the tortillas into small squares, deep fry them in hot oil until golden brown. Drain well. Pour the liquid from the tomatoes into a blender. Remove the tough skins from the tomatoes and add the pulp to the blender. Add garlic and blend until all is pureed. Cook the onion in 2 Tbsp. fat until wilted. Add the pureed tomatoes, tortillas and 1/2 a cup of the chicken stock. Salt and pepper to taste. Cover and cook over low heat, without stirring, for 30 minutes. Pour half the sauce into an earthenware casserole. Sprinkle with 1 cup of cheese. Arrange chicken over this and pour remaining sauce over all. Blend the sour cream with the 3 Tbsp. heavy cream and pour over the casserole. Add the remaining cheese, cream and chicken stock. Bake 30 minutes or until cheese is melted and casserole bubbles.

*Serves 6*

**PFEIFER HOUSE**
760 River Road (P.O. Box 471)
Tahoe City, CA   95730
(916) 583-3102
Hours:  6:00 p.m. - 10:00 p.m.  Closed Tuesday
Credit Cards:  All major
Prices:  Moderate
Reservations:  Suggested
Specialties:  Old European, Continental

*The Pfeifer House is a tradition to long-time Tahoe residents and vacationers, a place they must splurge on at least once a season, for their taste buds call to them, "Pfeifer House, take me to the Pfeifer House." The building itself, an illegal gambling house in the '40s, is Old Tahoe. It is full of pictures of the Alps and hung with authentic artifacts belonging to its German owners, Franz Fassbender and Henry Obermuller.  They are also the cooks and the creators of the magnificent recipes for sauerbraten, schnitzel, koenigsberger klopse and the incomparable potato pancakes.  The service is perfect, the food a series of masterpieces.  Don't miss this stop.*

175

# Pfeifer House Salad Dressing

| | |
|---|---|
| 1 | whole egg or 3 Tbsp. mayonnaise |
| 1/8 | c. white wine vinegar or tarragon vinegar |
| 1/8 | c. red wine vinegar |
| 1/4 | tsp. dry mustard |
| 1/4 | tsp. Dijon mustard |
| 1/4 | tsp. salt |
| 1/8 | tsp. white pepper |
| 1/4 | tsp. tarragon |
| 1/8 | tsp. sugar |
| 1/4 | tsp. Swiss Knorr Aromat |
| | few drops Maggi |
| 1 | c. oil |

Place all ingredients except oil in a food processor.  Gradually add the oil, blending until creamy.

*Makes 12 oz*

# Duckling a la Orange

| | |
|---|---|
| 1 | 4 to 5 lb. duckling |
| 1 | 10-oz. can condensed milk chicken broth |
| 1 | c. orange juice |
| 1 | c. Grand Marnier |
| 2 | Tbsp. cornstarch |
| 1 | Tbsp. honey |
| 1 | Tbsp. lemon juice rind of 2 oranges, grated orange sections |

On rack in a shallow baking pan, roast duckling at 325° F. for 2 to 2 1/2 hours.  Meanwhile, in a saucepan, combine remaining ingredients except the orange rind and sections.  Cook until thickened, stirring constantly.  Remove duckling, pour off fat, stir sauce into drippings in baking pan.  Add orange rind.  Cut duckling into serving size pieces and arrange on serving plate.  Pour some sauce over top, garnish with orange sections, serve remaining sauce on the side.

*Serves 4*

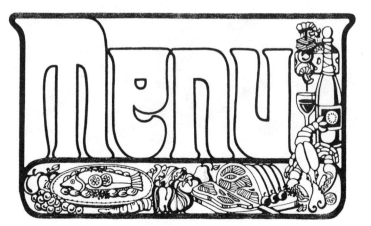

# Geschnetzeltes Veal

| | |
|---|---|
| 1 1/2 | lbs. veal, sliced into strips 1/4" thick and 2" long |
| 1/4 | c. butter |
| 1 | c. dry white wine |
| 10 | oz. demi-glace (see glossary) |
| 1/2 | c. light cream |
| 1/3 | c. sour cream |
| 1 | Tbsp. lemon juice |
| 2 | Tbsp. parsley, chopped |
| 1 | c. fresh mushrooms, sliced |
| | salt and pepper to taste |
| | paprika to taste |

Saute veal in butter until golden brown. Add white wine and simmer until wine is almost absorbed. Add demi-glace, cream and sour cream. Simmer and stir in lemon juice, parsley and mushrooms. Season to taste. Serve with spaetzle. (see page 103)

*Serves 4*

# German Applestrudel

*Dough:*

| | |
|---|---|
| 3 | c. flour, sifted |
| 1/4 | tsp. salt |
| 1 | egg, beated |
| 1 | Tbsp. oil |
| 1 | c. water, lukewarm |
| 1 | c. butter, melted and cooled |
| 1/2 | c. flour |
| | oil |

*Filling:*

| | |
|---|---|
| 4 | medium apples, pared, cored, cut into 1/8" thick slices |
| 2 | Tbsp. vanilla extract |
| 4 | Tbsp. sugar |
| 1 | tsp. cinnamon |
| 1/2 | tsp. allspice |
| | juice of 1 lemon |
| 5 | Tbsp. raisins |

In a large bowl, combine flour and salt. Blend in the egg and oil. Stir constantly. Gradually add the water. Mix until a soft dough is formed. Turn dough onto a lightly floured board. Hold dough above board and hit it against the board approximately 100 times. Knead slightly and pat into a ball. Lightly brush the top with oil. Cover dough with an inverted bowl and allow it to rest for 30 minutes. On a 40" x 30" table, place a clean cloth, allowing it to hand down. Sprinkle (mostly in the center) the cloth with flour. Place dough in center and roll it into a 12" square. If necessary, sprinkle more flour under dough. Lightly brush off flour on top and brush top with cooking oil.

## German Applestrudel (Cont.)

With palms of hands down, reach under the dough to the center and lift slightly, being careful not to tear the dough. To stretch, gently and steadily pull arms in opposite directions. Keep pulling and stretching dough, until it is tissue paper thin and hangs over the edges of the table on all sides. Trim off thick outer edges.

Allow stretched dough to dry 10 minutes. Avoid drying too long as it becomes brittle. Drizzle dough with 1/4 c. butter. For the filling, place apples in a sauce pan. Add vanilla extract, sugar, cimmanon, allspice, lemon juice and raisins. Bring to a boil and cool. Place the filling onto the dough. Fold three sides of the overhanging dough over the filling. Drizzle filling with 1/2 c. butter. Beginning at narrow folded end, grasp the cloth with hands, holding it taut. Slowly lift the cloth and roll dough over the filling. Pull the cloth towards you, again lift cloth and holding it taut, slowly and loosely roll the dough. Cut strudel into halves. Lifting each half on cloth, gently roll each onto a generously buttered baking sheet. Brush off excess flour. Cut off end of roll. Brush top and sides of strudel with some of the butter. Bake at 350° F. 35 to 45 minutes or until strudels are golden brown. Remove to cooling rack. Sift confectioners sugar over top. Cut strudels into 2" pieces.

*Makes 2 Strudels*

180

# Pierce Street Annex

### PIERCE STREET ANNEX
7375 Lighthouse Center behind Safeway, (P. O. Box 7375)
Tahoe City, CA  95730
(916) 583-5800
Hours:  11:30 a.m. - 3:00 p.m. Daily, lunch
5:30 p.m. - 10:30 p.m. Daily, dinner
Until 1 a.m. - Limited menu
10:00 a.m. - 3:00 p.m. Sunday brunch
Credit Cards:  American Express, Visa, Mastercard
Prices:  Inexpensive to moderate
Reservations:  Suggested
Specialties:  American Cuisine

*Pierce Street Annex is part of a coast-to-coast network of restaurants whose first location was opened in 1962 on Pierce Street in San Francisco. Owner Marty Davis and partners eventually expanded to Alaska, the East Coast, Southern California and now Lake Tahoe.*

*Despite all the trendy, nouveau cuisines that catapulted into favor - and disfavor - during the 26 years of Pierce Street Annex expansion, the restaurants have steadfastly stuck to good old American fare. As a result they have become adept at a restaurant's basic duty - namely, to feed people good food at a reasonable price and send them home filled instead of hungry. This philosophy, coupled with the Annex's ability to create a warm, comfortable dining room complete with blazing fireplace, friendly faces, quick and cheery service, plus the food like Mom used to cook, makes dining at Pierce Street Annex on Tahoe's North Shore a nostalgic gastronomic treat.*

181

# Escargot Butter

1/4    c. parsley, chopped
8      cloves garlic, chopped
1/2    lb. butter, melted
1      oz. Pernod or anisette
       sprinkle of caraway seed
       dash or two of Tabasco
6      escargot
       French bread, cubed

Place parsley and garlic in saute pan with butter. Add all the other ingredients and simmer for 20 minutes, stirring frequently. Pour over escargot in their dishes and broil for approximately 8 to 10 minutes. Serve with warm cubed French bread.

*Serves 8*

# Meatloaf Hungarian Style

| | |
|---|---|
| 1 | large onion, chopped |
| 2 | cloves garlic, chopped |
| 1/3 | bunch parsley, chopped |
| 2 | lbs. ground pork |
| 1 | lb. ground veal |
| 2 | lbs. ground beef |
| 2 | eggs |
| 1 | Tbsp. Worcestershire Sauce |
| 1 | Tbsp. paprika |
| 1 | c. milk |
| 1 | tsp. each of celery salt, pepper and savory salt |
| 6 | strips bacon |

Mix together all ingredients except bacon. Form into loaf and place in baking pan with strips of bacon on top. Bake at 400° F. for 35 minutes. Raise temperature to 475° F. and bake an additional 15 minutes. Allow to cool before removing from the pan.

*Serves 8*

# Lemon Mustard Chicken

| | |
|---|---|
| 4 | Tbsp. butter |
| 1 | Tbsp. lemon juice |
| | pinch of ground white pepper |
| 1 | tsp. Dijon mustard |
| 3 | Tbsp. sour cream |
| 8 | boneless chicken breasts, sauteed or |
| 8 | veal steaks, sauteed |

Melt butter, add lemon juice, pepper and mustard. Place over medium heat, stirring constantly for about 1 minute. Add sour cream and raise heat to medium high. Stir another minute. Pour over sauteed chicken breasts or veal.

*Serves 8*

# RESTAURANT • BAR

**THE PINES**
Hyatt Lake Tahoe
Lakeshore Boulevard and Country Club Drive (P.O. Box 3239)
Incline Village, NV   89450
(702) 831-1111
Hours:  6 p.m. to 10 p.m. Sunday - Thursday
6 p.m. to 11 p.m. Friday and Saturday
10:00 a.m. - 2:00 p.m.  Sunday Champagne Brunch
Credit Cards:  All major
Prices:  Moderate to expensive
Reservations:  Recommended
Specialties:  Continental with Pasta, Seafood and Steaks

*The Pines is elegant. With its contemporary decor in pinks and deep forest green, its absolutely lovely pink morning glory china, the secluded booths and etched-glass windows - what a treat to be served in style. The Pines concentrates on international specialties, and the freshest available seafood specials change daily. The Sunday brunch is a sight to behold, even if you're not hungry, for the ice sculptures take your breath away. But with made-to-order omelettes, the sweetest desserts this side of Vienna, and endless champagne, there's a lot more than just ice carvings to please you.*

185

# Prawns Italiano

| | |
|---|---|
| 3 | jumbo prawns, shelled and cleaned |
| 3 | slices prosciutto ham, sliced not too thin |
| | olive oil |
| 1 | garlic clove, chopped |
| 1 | shallot, chopped |
| 1/2 | c. white wine |
| 2 | leaves fresh basil, chopped |
| 1/2 | tomato, peeled, seeded and diced |
| 1 | oz. butter |
| | fresh ground pepper |

Wrap the prawns in the sliced prosciutto. Saute prawns in hot olive oil. When they are halfway done, add garlic and shallots. When the prawns are finished, remove from the pan and keep warm. Add the white wine and reduce liquid by half. Add basil and tomato. Blend butter into the reduced sauce. Add pepper to taste and pour the sauce over the prawns.

*Serves 1*

## PRIMAVERA
Caesar's Tahoe Casino
Highway 50 at Stateline (P.O. Box 5800)
Stateline, NV 89449
(702) 588-3515
Hours: 6:00 p.m. - 11:00 p.m. Dinner, Wednesday - Saturday
10:00 a.m. - 3:00 p.m. Brunch, Saturday and Sunday
Credit Cards: All major
Prices: Moderate to expensive
Reservations: Recommended
Specialties: Italian

*The beautiful Primavera is located inside the luxurious Caesar's Spa and features canopied tables reminiscent of elegant outdoor European cafes. It specializes in authentic Italian cuisine, and offerings include fresh pasta, pizza, fresh seafood, veal, salads and more, all complemented with tantalizing pastries. The Primavera is surrounded by a lagoon-type swimming pool and a backdrop of natural splendor, making this indoor/outdoor setting the most distinctive in the area.*

# Minestrone A la Milanese

| | |
|---|---|
| 1 | slice salt pork |
| 1 | lb. fresh peas, unshelled |
| 1 | lb. fresh borlotti beans, or cranberry beans |
| 2 | Tbsp. fresh parsley, chopped |
| 1 | small bunch basil, chopped |
| 2 | fresh sage leaves, chopped |
| 1 | onion, chopped |
| 1 | clove garlic, minced |
| 2 | strips bacon |
| 1/4 | c. butter |
| 1 | carrot, finely chopped |
| 1 | stalk celery, finely chopped |
| 1 1/2 | c. tomatoes, peeled, seeded and chopped |
| 2 | small zucchini, finely chopped |
| 4 | strips pancetta bacon, cut in 1/2" pieces |
| 7 1/2 | c. boiling water |
| | salt to taste |
| 2 | potatoes, peeled and sliced |
| 1/2 | c. rice |
| 1 | head savoy cabbage, shredded |
| | salt and pepper to taste |
| 5 | Tbsp. Parmesan cheese, grated |

Place salt pork in a pan of cold water and boil for 5 minutes, then plunge it into cold water and let it cool. Cut into strips. Shell peas and beans and put them in separate bowls of cold water. In a large saute pan, place parsley, basil, sage, onion, garlic, bacon and 2 tablespoons of the butter. Add carrot, celery, tomatoes and zucchii.

## Minestrone A la Milanese (Cont.)

Add pancetta and cook, stirring often, until onion has softened and bacon is partially cooked. Add boiling water, salt lightly, and bring back to boil. Add the drained beans and pork, stir and cook for 2 hours. Add potatoes, rice, cabbage and drained peas. Cook uncovered until rice is al dente (see glossary), stirring often. Be careful not to overcook rice, remembering it will continue to cook in the hot soup when removed from the heat. Season to taste with salt and pepper, swirl in remaining 2 tablespoons butter and 1 tablespoon Parmesan. Allow to cook. Ladle into soup bowls and dust with remaining Parmesan. Serve cool or cold, but not chilled.

*Serves 4*

# Spaghetti Con Le Vongole

| | |
|---|---|
| 2 1/2 | lbs. clams |
| 2 | cloves garlic, crushed |
| 1/4 | c. olive oil |
| 2 1/2 | lbs. ripe tomatoes, peeled, seeded and chopped |
| | pepper |
| 1 | lb. spaghetti |
| 2 | Tbsp. fresh parsley, chopped |

Wash clams thoroughly, rinsing away any sand. If possible, let them soak in cold salted water for 1 to 2 hours. Put them in a large pan, cover and cook over low heat, shaking occasionally, until all clams are open. Remove clams from their shells and transfer to a bowl. (If they still seem to have sand in them, rinse in lukewarm water.) Strain clam-cooking liquid through cheesecloth and set aside. Fry garlic in oil until lightly browned. Add tomatoes, clam liquid and a pinch of pepper, and cook over high heat, stirring often. Cook spaghetti in plenty of boiling salted water until al dente (see glossary). A minute before pasta is done, add clams and parsley to tomato mixture, bring to a boil and remove from heat immediately. Drain pasta, transfer to a serving dish, mix in sauce and serve immediately.

*Serves 4*

**RIVER RANCH**

Alpine Meadows Road and Highway 89 (P.O. Box 197)

Tahoe City, CA   95730

(916) 583-4264

Hours:  11:30 a.m. - 5:00 p.m. Lunch, summers only

5:30 p.m. - 10:30 p.m. Dinner, daily

Credit Cards:  All major

Prices:  Moderate

Reservations:  Recommended, especially on weekends

Specialties:  Fresh Fish, Steak, Veal, Duck, Wild Game

*One of the area's most popular restaurants in both summer and winter is the cedar-shingled lodge called the River Ranch, located on the banks of the Truckee River. The new dining room, cantilevered over the rushing rapids, provides a breathtaking setting. Specialties of the house include roast duck with seasoned brandied fresh fruit sauces, rack of lamb, and pepper steak. The seafood selections always seem to be the freshest around and are prepared with complementary sauces that guarantee satisfaction. The chef also prepares a special from the wild game list each evening. For dessert, try the magnificent Creme Brulee Tart or "River Ranch Coupe," a combination of vanilla ice cream, fresh strawberries and Grand Marnier.*

191

# Roast Duck Montmorency

| | |
|---|---|
| 1 | duck |

*Sauce:*

| | |
|---|---|
| 5 | oz. dark sweet cherries and juice |
| 5 | oz. mandarin oranges and juice |
| 1/4 | c. beef or duck gravy |
| 1 | oz. cornstarch |
| 1 | oz. brandy |
| | fresh parsley, chopped |

Cut duckling in 1/2 and roast in 450 oven for 2 hours or until golden brown. Debone ribs from duck's chest. For the sauce, add cherries and oranges in sauce pan, simmer to rolling boil and add gravy. Stir gently so as not to break up oranges and cherries. Add cornstarch to thicken. Add brandy to taste. Ladle sauce on top of duck. Garnish with chopped parsley.

*Serves 2*

# Tournedos de Venison with Two Sauces

| | |
|---|---|
| 4 | 4-oz. tournedo |
| 1 | Tbsp. olive oil |
| 1 | Tbsp. butter |
| 1 | round crouton |

Season meat and saute in olive oil and butter. Fry crouton and place on plate. Top with meat and coat 1/2 with Sauce Dijonaise (recipe follows) and 1/2 with Sauce au Poivre (recipe follows).

*Serves 2*

# Sauce Dijonaise

| | |
|---|---|
| 4 | c. white wine |
| 5 | shallots, chopped |
| 2 | mushrooms, chopped |
| 2 | c. veloute (see glossary) |
| 3 | c. cream |
| | salt and pepper to taste |
| 2 - 4 | Tbsp. Dijon mustard |
| 1/2 | oz. butter |

Combine wine, shallots and mushrooms and reduce by 2/3. Add veloute and cream, season with salt and pepper. Reduce to a light nappe and strain. Add mustard to taste and moisten with butter.

# Sauce au Poivre

| | |
|---|---|
| 3 | 1/2-oz. carrots, finely chopped |
| 3 | 1-oz. onions, finely chopped |
| | parsley stems |
| | thyme |
| | bay leaf |
| 1 | Tbsp. butter |
| 1/2 | c. red wine vinegar |
| 1 | c. red wine |
| 4 1/2 | c. demi-glace (see glossary) |
| 24 | peppercorns |
| 1 | Tbsp. butter |

Saute vegetables and spices in butter until light-brown. Deglaze with vinegar and red wine. Reduce by 2/3. Add demi-glace and peppercorns and reduce. Strain. Add butter.

# Breast of Pheasant with Sauce Madeira

2 1/2    c. brown sauce (see glossary)
1/4      c. Madeira
2        Tbsp. truffles, minced
          salt and pepper to taste
2        pheasants, cleaned
1/2      lemon
          salt and pepper to taste
4        Tbsp. butter

In sauce pan heat brown sauce. Simmer until reduced 1/4 and add the Madeira and truffles. Add salt and pepper. Preheat oven to 350. Rub lemon inside and outside 2 ready-to-cook pheasants. Season inside and out with salt and pepper. In heavy pan, heat butter and brown the birds on all sides. Place pan in the oven. Roast for about 30 minutes, basting every 10 minutes. Remove birds and cool slightly. Remove the breast from the birds and slice thinly. Fan the slices along the curve of the plate. Cover lightly with sauce.

*Serves 4*

# Mango Sorbet

2        15-oz. jars mangoes in syrup
1        tsp. fresh lemon juice

Combine undrained mangoes and lemon juice in food processor until smooth. Turn mixture into bowl and refrigerate. Transfer mixture to ice cream maker and process.

*Serves 8*

# Strawberry Mousse

| | |
|---|---|
| 2 | egg whites at room temperature |
| 1/4 | tsp. cream of tartar |
| | pinch of salt |
| 2 | c. whipping cream |
| 1 1/4 | c. powdered sugar |
| 2 | c. strawberries, pureed and chilled |
| | whipped cream |

Beat egg whites, cream of tartar and salt in small bowl until stiff and glossy. Whip cream with sugar in medium bowl until stiff. Whisk strawberry puree into cream until mixture is very thick. Gently fold in egg whites, blending well. Spoon mousse into champagne glasses. Refrigerate at least 1 hour. Garnish with whipped cream just before serving.

*Serves 10*

# Creme Brulee Berry Tart

| | |
|---|---|
| 5 | Tbsp. sugar |
| 7 | egg yolks |
| 2 | c. cream |
| 1 | c. sour cream |
| 1 | tsp. vanilla |
| 2 | Tbsp. butter |
| 1 | pie crust, baked and cooled |
| | chocolate sauce |
| | fresh raspberries |
| | brown sugar |

## Creme Brulee Berry Tart (Cont.)

On low heat in a double boiler whisk sugar and egg yolks together. Add cream, sour cream and vanilla. Stir with wooden spoon. Simmer until thick drops form on spoon. Remove from heat. Stir in butter. Let cool at room temperature. Coat bottom crust with a thin layer of chocolate sauce. Add raspberries to cover bottom. Place the cooled cream filling on top. Refrigerate until firm. Sprinkle with brown sugar and place under broiler until light brown. Cool again for 5 minutes, slice and serve.

*Serves 12*

**SCHAFFER'S MILL**

Northstar-at-Tahoe

Mailing address: P. O. Box 129

Truckee, CA 95734

(916) 562-1010

Hours: Call for current hours

Credit Cards: Mastercard, Visa, American Express, Discover, Carte Blanche, Diners Club

Prices: Moderate

Reservations: Suggested

Specialties: California Cuisine

*This popular restaurant at the Northstar-at-Tahoe resort features a light California Cuisine using the freshest ingredients available, including fresh seafood daily, fresh vegetables, fresh herbs and spices, fresh sauces and freshly baked breads, pastries and desserts (baked on the premises by a full-time baker). The setting is in the tradition of old San Francisco restaurants, giving Schaffer's Mill a casually elegant atmosphere. A variety of entrees that change with the seasons gives diners new choices as well as the traditional fare. A broad selection of fine California varietal wines to complement the cuisine is offered, all reasonably priced. Live entertainment is featured on weekends at the piano in the adjoining bar and lounge.*

# Teriyaki Sauce

| | |
|---|---|
| 2 | c. soy sauce |
| 1 | c. brown sugar |
| 1 | c. white vinegar |
| 1 | c. pineapple juice |
| 1 | tsp. garlic powder |
| 1/2 | tsp. salt |
| 2 | tsp. sherry |

Combine ingredients in saucepan. Bring to boil and simmer 20 minutes. Use as a marinade for teriyaki steaks and chicken.

*Yields 5 cups*

# Tomatillo and Cilantro Sauce

| | |
|---|---|
| 2 | lbs. tomatillos |
| 6 | Serrano chilies |
| 1 | c. white wine |
| 2 | Tbsp. diced shallots |
| | juice from 2 fresh limes |
| 1 | large bunch cilantro |

In a pot cook tomatillos, Serrano chilies, white wine, shallots and lime juice for 10 minutes. Transfer to blender. Add cilantro and puree. Ideal served over grilled swordfish.

*Makes 8-10 servings*

# Tempura Shrimp or Vegetables

| | |
|---|---|
| 2 | c. flour |
| 1/2 | tsp. salt |
| 1/8 | c. sugar |
| 1 | tsp. baking powder |
| 2 | eggs |
| 1 1/2 | c. water |

Mix dry ingredients. Beat together eggs and water. Add to dry ingredients and beat until smooth. Refrigerate. Coat shrimp, fish or vegetables with batter and deep fry until golden brown.

*Yields 3 1/2 cups*

# Poached Salmon with Kiwi Beurre Blanc

| 2 | lbs. salmon fillets |
| 1 | c. water |
| 1/2 | c. white wine |
| 1/2 | c. cream |
| 2 | Tbsp. shallots, diced |
| | juice from 1 fresh lemon |
| 4 | kiwis, peeled and sliced |
| 1/2 | lb. butter, cut in pieces |

Preheat oven to 400°F . Portion salmon into 4-ounce pieces. Place in shallow baking pan with water. Bake 8-10 minutes. While salmon is cooking place wine, cream, shallots, lemon juice and 3 kiwis in a pot. Cook and reduce to about 1/4 cup liquid. Transfer liquid and cooked kiwi to blender. Add butter by piece to the liquid, blending at low speed. Place salmon fillets on plate. Pour sauce over salmon, and garnish with remaining kiwi.

*Serves 8*

# Poached Orange Roughy with Jalapeno Fruit Sauce

| 4 | 6-oz. orange roughy fillets |
| 1 | c. beer |
| 2 | large jalapeno peppers, minced |
| 1 | Tbsp. shallots, minced |
| 2 | Tbsp. lemon juice |
| 1 | c. cream |
| 1 | c. fish stock |

## Poached Orange Roughy with Jalapeno Fruit Sauce (cont.)

1 1/2   Tbsp. cornstarch
1/2     c. strawberries, sliced
1/2     c. blueberries
1/2     c. nectarines, sliced
1/2     c. grapes, cut in half

Poach orange roughy fillets in beer until they are no longer transparent. In a sauce pan, combine jalapeno peppers, shallots, lemon juice, cream and fish stock. Bring to a boil and reduce to a simmer, cooking until reduced by half. Thicken with cornstarch. Add fruit and pour on top of the fish.

*Serves 4*

# Peanut Butter Pie

*Crust:*

| | |
|---|---|
| 1 | box Nabisco Chocolate Wafer Cookies |
| | melted butter |

*Filling:*

| | |
|---|---|
| 8 | oz. cream cheese, softened |
| 1 | c. creamy peanut butter |
| 1 | c. powdered sugar |
| 1 | pt. whipping cream |
| 1 | generous splash Kahlua |

*Topping:*

| | |
|---|---|
| 8 | oz. semi-sweet chocolate, melted |
| | water |
| | chopped roasted peanuts |

Crush chocolate wafers and add a small amount of melted butter until wafers are moist. Pat into pie tin to form a crust. Bake for 5 minutes at 350° F. to set. Refrigerate until ready for filling. Mix cream cheese, peanut butter and powdered sugar with fork until smooth. Whip cream, reserving enough for decorations. Slowly fold whipped cream into peanut butter mixture and at the same time add the Kahlua. Be gentle to achieve a light yet rich blend. Fill pie crust then refrigerate while working on topping. Melt chocolate and whip in a bit of water until spreading consistency (fairly thick). Spread over pie. Using pastry bag with star tip, decorate the pie with reserved whipped cream. Sprinkle with chopped roasted peanuts. Refrigerate for at least an hour before serving.

*Serves 8*

# Fresh California Avocado Chiffon Pie

| | |
|---|---|
| 1 | envelope unflavored gelatin |
| 6 | Tbsp. sugar |
| 2 | eggs separated |
| 1 1/2 | c. milk |
| 1 | ripe avocado mashed |
| 1/4 | c. fresh lemon juice |
| 1/2 | pt. whipping cream |
| 1 | prepared graham cracker or regular crust |

In saucepan mix gelatin with 4 Tablespoons of the sugar. Blend egg yolks with milk and add to gelatin mixture. Let stand 1 minute. Stir over low heat until gelatin and sugar are dissolved. With a wire whip blend in avocado and lemon juice. Pour into bowl and chill. Beat egg whites, adding the other 2 tablespoons of sugar until stiff. Gently fold egg whites into avocado/gelatin mixture. Place in prepared crust and chill until firm (at least 1 hour). Brush pie with additional lemon juice to retain bright green color. Garnish with whipped cream.

*Serves 8*

**SEAFARE AT HARRAH'S**
Headliner Building
219 No. Center Street (P.O. Box 10)
Reno, NV 89520
(702) 786-3232
Hours: 11:30 a.m. - 5:00 p.m. Lunch
5:00 p.m. - 11:00 p.m. Sunday through Thursday
5:00 p.m. - 11:00 p.m. Friday and Saturday
Credit Cards: All major
Prices: Moderate
Reservations: Recommended
Specialties: Seafood

*The nautical theme of the Seafare includes ship rigging, high carved-wood ceilings and an unlikely spacious and roomy feeling not to be found on any sailing ship of old. Hurricane lamps light each table - in case of a nor'wester? Ships' figureheads, carved from wood and mounted on the vertical beams, lend even more of an old salty touch. The seafood here is excellent, of course, living up to the nautical "flavor" of the surroundings.*

# Oriental Seafood Salad

*Salad ingredients:*

| | |
|---|---|
| 12 | oz. bay shrimps |
| 2 | heads bibb lettuce |
| 8 | oz. calamari, cooked and julienned |
| 2 | Tbsp. sesame seeds |

*Mild Szechuan Dressing:*

| | |
|---|---|
| 1 | heaping Tbsp. hoisin sauce* |
| 2 | Tbsp. soy sauce |
| 2 | Tbsp. rice vinegar* |
| 1 | tsp. sesame oil* |
| | dash Tabasco sauce |
| | scallions, julienned |

Toss salad ingredients.  Mix together hoisin sauce, soy sauce, rice vinegar, sesame oil and Tabasco sauce.  Toss together with the salad ingredients and garnish with julienne of scallions.

*Available in Oriental markets

*Serves 4*

# Chicken Breast Frambois

| | |
|---|---|
| 1 | pt. fresh raspberries |
| 2 | oz. unsalted butter |
| 5 | oz. vodka |
| | sugar to taste |
| | salt and pepper to taste |
| 1/2 | c. heavy cream |
| 4 | 7-oz. chicken breasts, skinned |
| 1/2 | c. flour |
| 4 | oz. butter |

Puree raspberries in blender, strain if desired. Add unsalted butter, vodka, sugar, salt and pepper. Bring to a quick boil, add cream and blend. Slightly flatten chicken breasts, trim if necessary, and dredge them in flour. In butter, melted to a nutty brown, saute chicken until done.

*Serves 4*

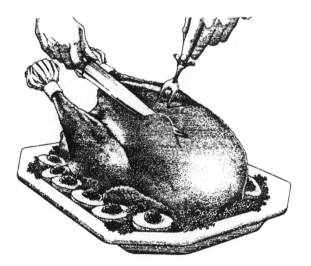

# Dungeness Crabcakes

| | |
|---|---|
| 4 | c. crabmeat |
| 2 | Tbsp. onions, finely chopped |
| 2 | Tbsp. celery, finely chopped |
| 2 | tsp. Worcestershire Sauce |
| | salt to taste |
| | white pepper to taste |
| 1/2 | c. milk |
| 4 | Tbsp. parsley, finely chopped |
| 1 | c. fresh bread crumbs |
| 2 | tsp. white wine |
| 3 | eggs, beaten |
| 8 | Tbsp. butter |

*Sauce:*

| | |
|---|---|
| 1 | c. salad oil |
| 1/3 | c. red wine vinegar |
| | salt and pepper |
| 2 | tsp. fresh ginger, finely minced |
| 1 | Tbsp. onions, chopped |
| 1/2 | c. fresh coriander |
| 1 | Tbsp. sugar |
| | pinch of garlic powder |

Blend and mix first 11 ingredients. Melt 1 tablespoon butter and add it to the mixture. Shape into 12 cakes and fry in melted butter until golden brown, about 6 to 7 minutes. For the sauce, blend remaining ingredients in blender for about 30 seconds. Heat and pour over crabcakes.

*Serves 6*

**SIR CHARLES FINE DINING**
Cal Neva Lodge and Casino (P. O. Box 368)
Crystal Bay, NV 89402
(702) 832-4000
Hours: 6:00 p.m. - 10:00 p.m. Tuesday - Sunday
Credit Cards: All major
Prices: Moderate
Reservations: Recommended
Specialties: Continental Cuisine

*The on-going refurbishment of the Cal Neva Casino in Crystal Bay - the respected and beautiful Lady of the Lake - which began in January of 1986 and continues, has resulted in a plush spot to gamble, indulge in a drink with a spectacular view, or dine in a posh restaurant. Sir Charles combines sophistication with a touch of rustic mountain decor - designed by owner Charles Bluth - and serves the classy foods expected in a fine-dining establishment. Chef Eric Laslow takes great pride in his dishes, which are also visual works of art. The food is rich and filling and Sir Charles is developing a reputation as the in place to dine.*

# Court Bouillon

| | |
|---|---|
| 1 | qt. water |
| 1/4 | c. lemon juice |
| 1/2 | c. rice wine vinegar |
| 1/2 | c. red wine |
| 1 | medium onion, quartered |
| 1 | stalk celery |
| 5 | sprigs parsley |
| 1 | tsp. black pepper |
| 24 | large prawns |

Combine first 8 ingredients and bring to a boil. Add prawns and simmer until just firm. Remove prawns and chill in ice water. The remaining broth (court bouillon) may be saved or frozen for poaching any seafood items in the future.

# Vinaigrette

| | |
|---|---|
| 3 | Tbsp. Dijon mustard |
| 1 | egg |
| 1/2 | c. rice wine vinegar |
| 4 | cloves roasted garlic, peeled (Rub garlic clove in olive oil and place in 350° oven. Roast until golden brown) |
| 4 | sprigs cilantro |
| 3 | oz. fresh ginger, peeled and sliced |
| 5 | serrano chilies, roasted and peeled |
| 1/2 | c. olive oil |
| 1/2 | c. sesame oil |
| | salt and pepper to taste |

Combine all ingredients, stir thoroughly, refrigerate.

# Sir Charles Salad

| | |
|---|---|
| 1 | bunch spinach, rinsed and dried |
| 2 | oz. snow peas, julienned |
| 1/2 | red bell pepper, julienned |
| 4 | green onions, julienned |
| 1/2 | gold bell pepper, julienned |

*Dressing:*

| | |
|---|---|
| 2 | oz. sesame oil |
| 3 | oz. swordfish, cut into bite-sized pieces |
| 3 | oz. ahi tuna, cut into bite-sized pieces |
| 4 | oz. white wine |
| 2 | oz. raspberry vinegar |
| | rind of 1 lemon |
| | juice of 1 lemon |

Assemble salad ingredients in large bowl and set aside. In medium saute pan over medium heat add sesame oil and seafood. Saute until partially done. Lower heat. Add wine and vinegar, simmer and reduce by half while turning the seafood occasionally. Add lemon rind and juice. Add seafood mixture to salad and toss.

*Serves 2*

# Seafood Bisque & Curried Sesame Butter

*Butter:*

| | |
|---|---|
| 1/2 | c. butter |
| 1 | Tbsp. toasted sesame seeds |
| 2 | Tbsp. curry powder |
| 1 | c. green onions, finely diced |
| 1 | tsp. lemon juice |
| 2 | sprigs dill, chopped |
| 2 | cloves garlic |

In food processor combine all ingredients and blend until smooth. Butter may be rolled into a long log shape on parchment paper and wrapped. Set aside and chill.

*Bisque:*

| | |
|---|---|
| 1/4 | c. clarified butter (see glossary) |
| 4 | anchovy fillets |
| 1/4 | c. fresh basil, chopped |
| 3 | oz. scallops, cut into bite-sized pieces |
| 3 | oz. prawns, cut into bite-sized pieces |
| 3 | oz. lobster, cut into bite-sized pieces |
| 1 | red bell pepper, diced |
| 2 | Tbsp. shallots, minced |
| 3/4 | c. brandy |
| 1 | c. white wine |
| 1 | c. whipping cream |

## Seafood Bisque & Curried Sesame Butter (Cont.)

Warm clarified butter in medium sauce pan and add next 7 ingredients, saute over medium heat for approximately 5 minutes. Remove from heat and add brandy and wine. Heat slowly. As mixture begins to bubble, add cream and simmer until a creamy consistency is achieved, approximately 5-10 minutes.

Serve piping hot with a slice of curried sesame butter on top. If you have butter left over it freezes very well and may be used to serve over fish or other soups.

*Serves 4*

# Salmon with Saffron and Caviar Cream

| | |
|---|---|
| 1 | oz. olive oil |
| 1 | tsp. shallots, minced |
| 1 | c. white wine |
| 1 | oz. lime juice |
| 1 | oz. rice wine vinegar |
| 1 | tsp. balsamic vinegar |
| 1 | c. whipping cream or manufacturing cream |
|   | pinch saffron |
| 2 | Tbsp. red lumpfish caviar |
| 2 | 7-oz. portions salmon fillet, boned and skinned |

In medium saute pan over medium heat, add oil and saute shallots until soft (do not brown). Add wine, lime juice and vinegars. Heat to a mild boil and add cream, saffron and caviar. Mix well and place salmon in pan. Cover and reduce heat slightly and simmer until salmon is moderately firm. Remove and keep warm. Reduce sauce over medium heat until creamy. Serve over salmon.

*Serves 2*

# Fruit Crepes with Rum and Curry

| | |
|---|---|
| 1/2 | c. unsalted butter |
| 1 | c. brown sugar |
| 1 | c. Meyer's rum |
| 1 1/2 | Tbsp. curry powder |
| 1/2 | tsp. ground cloves |
| 1 1/2 | c. pineapple juice |
| 1 | Tbsp. cornstarch |
| 1 | c. pineapple, diced |
| 1 | c. seedless grapes |
| 1 | c. apricots, diced |
| 1 | c. bing cherries, pitted |
| 16 | crepes |

In sauce pan over medium heat melt butter and stir in sugar. Add rum, curry, cloves and 1 cup of the pineapple juice. Bring to a slow boil, simmer 5 minutes. In a bowl, mix cornstarch and remaining pineapple juice, stir into sauce. Add fruit and simmer until fruit is softened. If sauce becomes too thick, thin with more pineapple juice.

With a slotted spoon remove fruit from sauce, stuff crepes and roll them up. Cover with sauce and serve hot with vanilla ice cream, also delicious for breakfast over French toast.

*Serves 8*

**THE SOULE DOMAIN**
Stateline Rd., North Shore
Crystal Bay, NV  89403
Mailing address:  P. O. Box 1645, Kings Beach, CA 95719
(916) 546-7529
Hours:  6:00 p.m. - 10:00 p.m.
Credit Cards:  Visa, Mastercard American Express
Prices:  Moderate
Reservations:  Recommended
Specialties:  California Cuisine

*Formerly the Log Cabin, the Soule Domain boasts an innovative menu that changes to give guests some of the freshest seafood and seasonal California Cuisine available at the Noarth Shore.  Charlie Soule, the owner, has added many of this unique creations to the menu and has redecorated his log cabin, located on Stateline Road across from the Tahoe Biltmore, but has kept its genuine charm and rustic atmosphere.. The catchy name Soule Domain is the brainchild of chef Charlie, and he is  as clever with his cuisine as with the naming of the restaurant. Only good things can be said about every course - from the appetizers to the desserts, your "soul's" desire will be met.*

217

# Curry Vinaigrette

| | |
|---|---|
| 1 | egg yolk |
| 1 | Tbsp. Dijon mustard |
| 1 | c. olive oil |
| 1 | c. salad oil |
| 1/8 | c. sesame oil |
| 1 1/2 | Tbsp. curry powder |
| 1 1/2 | Tbsp. honey |
| 5 | oz. red wine vinegar |
| 1/2 | avocado |
| | salt and pepper |

Combine egg yolk and mustard. Blend all oils together, then add to yolk mixture slowly, whipping vigorously. Add approximately 2 c. oil or until you have achieved a mayonnaise-type consistency. In blender, combine remaining ingredients. With blender going, slowly add remaining oil until maximum thickness is achieved, then combine the mayonnaise and blender mixture.

*Yields 3 1/2 cups*

# Pesto Sauce

| | |
|---|---|
| 1 | c. fresh basil leaves |
| 1/2 | tomato |
| 2 | garlic cloves |
| 1/2 | c. grated Parmesan cheese |
| 1/2 | c. pine nuts or walnuts |
| | salt and pepper to taste |
| 1/4 | c. olive oil |
| 1 | c. white wine |
| 1/4 | c. sliced mushrooms |
| 1/4 | c. heavy cream |
| 1/8 | c. whipped butter |
| | cooked fettucine or other pasta |

Combine first 6 ingredients in food processor. Add olive oil slowly. Put in hot saute pan, add wine and mushrooms, reduce for 20 seconds over high heat, then add cream and reduce another 20 seconds. Finish with butter and serve with fettucine or other pasta.

*Serves 5*

# Banana Muffins

| | |
|---|---|
| 12 | c. whole wheat pastry flour |
| 8 | bananas |
| 2 | c. oil |
| 3 | c. honey |
| 4 | c. plain yogurt |
| 4 | c. apple juice |
| 8 | c. granola |
| 4 | tsp. baking powder |
| 4 | tsp. baking soda |
| 1 | Tbsp. vanilla |
| 4 | c. raisins |
| 24 | eggs |

Combine all ingredients in large bowl, then bake in muffin liners at 350° F. for 15 minutes.

*Serves a bunch!*

# Raspberry Cheesecake

| | |
|---|---|
| 1 1/2 | lb. cream cheese |
| 1 1/2 | c. sugar |
| 2 | whole eggs |
| 8 | oz. orange juice |
| 4 | oz. raspberry puree (fresh or frozen) |
| 3 | egg whites |

# Raspberry Cheesecake (Cont.)

*Crust:*

1       c. graham cracker crumbs
3       oz. butter

*Topping:*

8       oz. orange juice
4       oz. raspberry puree

Blend cream cheese in food processor. Add sugar and eggs, set aside. Reduce 8 oz. orange juice by half over high heat, add raspberry puree. Add this to the cream cheese. Remove from processor and fold in 3 egg whites beaten until stiff. Mix crumbs and butter together and form crust. Pour mixture into crust and bake 1 hour at 350° F. Turn oven off, but leave cake in for 10 minutes, then cool for 1 hour. Blend orange juice and raspberry puree and top cake with this mixture.

*Serves 10*

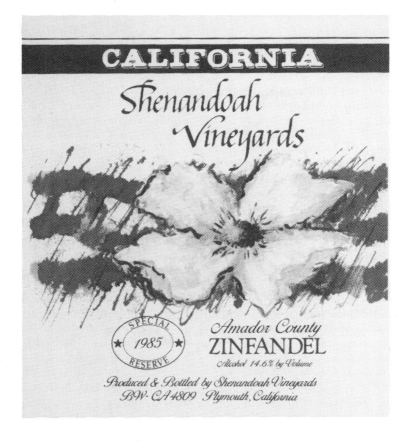

CALIFORNIA

Shenandoah Vineyards

SPECIAL 1985 RESERVE

Amador County
ZINFANDEL
Alcohol 14.6% by Volume

Produced & Bottled by Shenandoah Vineyards
BW-CA4809 Plymouth, California

The aromas are reminiscent of ripe blackberries, cherries and cocoa. The wine is full-bodied and only moderately tannic. It is beautifully structured with strong fruit and the high acid necessary for long ageing. The flavors are rich and complex and the finish very long and satisfying.

The wine is a perfect match for roasts, steak and rich sauces and will complement aged, full-flavored cheeses.

SQUEEZE IN
Commercial Row (P. O. Box 1001)
Truckee, CA   95734
(916) 587-9814
Hours:  7 a.m. - 2 p.m. Daily
Credit Cards:  None accepted
Prices:  Inexpensive
Reservations:  Not required
Specialties:  Omelettes

*Famous for its huge selection of omelettes, the Squeeze In on Truckee's famous Commercial Row has to rank high on anyone's list for good home cooking with generous portions for the hearty appetite. The only problem is choosing - there are 75 omelette creations on the menu, plus a list of other substantial meals for breakfast or lunch. Omelettes are sauteed in real butter and are huge.*

*The decor is definitely "Truckee funky," with memorabilia everywhere and a bygone-years, homey atmosphere. The service is quick and efficient. Eating at the Squeeze In is more than just eating out - it's an experience.*

# Dierdoni Omelette

| | |
|---|---|
| 3 | eggs, beaten |

*Filling:*

| | |
|---|---|
| 1/4 | c. sausage, diced |
| 1/4 | c. bacon, cooked and crumbled |
| 1 | tomato, chopped |
| 1/4 | c. mushrooms, chopped |
| 1/2 | c. Jack cheese, grated |

*Sauce:*

| | |
|---|---|
| 1 | Tbsp. butter |
| 1 | tsp. wine |

Cook 3 egg into an omelette. Set aside. Saute filling (everything but cheese). Combine sauce ingredients and stir into sauted filling. Sprinkle Jack cheese onto cooked omelette. Drain liquid off filling and pour filling into the cooked omelette. Fold over and serve.

*Serves 1*

# Huevos Mountana

| | |
|---|---|
| 1/2 | c. refried beans |
| 1 | corn tortilla |
| 1/2 | c. Jack cheese, grated |
| 2-4 | eggs |
| 1/2 | c. salsa |
| 1/2 | avocado, sliced |
| 1 | Tbsp. olives, chopped |
| | alfalfa sprouts |
| | sour cream |

### Huevos Mountana (Cont.)

In a saute pan spread refried beans on corn tortilla, sprinkle cheese on top and warm on low heat. In separate pan, fry 2-4 eggs, over easy. When eggs are cooked, put on top of tortilla, cover with salsa and remove from heat. Arrange avocados and olives on top. Sprinkle sprouts on top. Add a dollop of sour cream on top of it all.

*Serves 1*

# Fresh Salsa

| | |
|---|---|
| 1/2 | onion, chopped |
| 1 | carrot, chopped |
| 1/2 | bell pepper, chopped |
| 2-3 | jalapeno peppers, chopped |
| 1 | tsp. garlic powder |
| 1 | c. tomato sauce |
| 10 | fresh tomatoes, chopped |

Combine and mix all ingredients. Process half the mixture in a food processor. Add rest of the mixture and stir.

Variations may include adding fresh cilantro to taste or cooking the salsa down to a sauce.

*Yields 1 quart*

# Cream of Garden Vegetable Soup

| | |
|---|---|
| 1 | onion, finely chopped |
| 3-5 | carrots, diced small |
| 4 | Tbsp. butter |
| 2 | cloves fresh garlic, chopped |
| 2 | tsp. dill weed |
| | salt, pepper, oregano, basil, thyme, marjoram to taste |
| 8 | c. broth, chicken or vegetable |
| 1 | bunch broccoli, chopped |
| 1 | bunch spinach, chopped |
| 3-4 | zucchini, sliced thin |
| 1 | c. sour cream |
| 1 | c. half and half or milk |

In a stock pot saute onions and carrots in butter until onions are translucent. Add garlic, herbs and spices and stir until vegetables are coated. Add broth, bring to a boil. Add broccoli, spinach and zucchini and continue boiling until vegetables become tender. Cool and add sour cream and half and half or milk. Reheat slowly to serve. Serve with whole wheat toast squares and grated cheese on top.

*Serves 6-8*

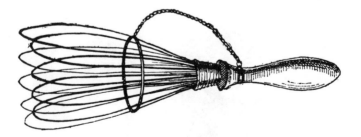

# Spinach Soup

| | |
|---|---|
| 1/4 | c. butter |
| 1 | clove garlic, chopped |
| 2 | Tbsp. fresh dill, chopped |
| 2 | bunches spinach |
| 1 | onion, chopped |
| 1/4 | c. flour |
| 4 | c. chicken broth |
| 2 | c. half and half |
| | salt and pepper to taste |
| 1 | grated carrot |

Melt butter in stock pot. Saute garlic for 2-3 minutes. Stir in dill, spinach and onion. Sprinkle with flour and stir again. Gradually blend in chicken broth. Cover and simmer for 10 minutes. Place in blender and puree. Return to pot and add half and half. Heat until bubbly and season to taste with salt and pepper. Garnish with grated carrot.

*Serves 10-12*

# Baca Bread Sandwich

| | |
|---|---|
| 2 | Tbsp. mayonnaise |
| 3 | slices French, rye or wheatberry bread |
| 3 | slices tomato |
| 3-4 | slices bacon, fried |
| 1/2 | avocado, sliced |
| 2 | slices cream cheese |
| | parsley |

Spread mayonnaise on 3 slices bread.  Place tomatoes on first slice and top with fried bacon.  Place another piece of bread on top, then avocado and 2 thick slices cream cheese.  Top with last piece of bread and garnish with parsley.

*Serves 1*

# *Stanley's*

STANLEY'S
941 Tahoe Blvd. (P. O. Box 3437)
Incline Village, NV   89450
(702) 831-9944
Hours:  8:00 a.m. - 11:45 a.m. Breakfast
11:45 a.m. - 2:30 p.m. Lunch
5:30 p.m. - 10:00 p.m. Dinner
Credit Cards:  Mastercard, Visa
Prices:  Moderate
Reservations:  Not required
Specialties:  Scampi, Spare Ribs, Fresh Seafood

*Stanley's in Incline Village is the oldest restaurant in that secluded little village. Owner Ginny Parsons, with the help of her kids, has run the cozy, intimate, and popular eatery for more years then we can remember. It is the place in town for the best Eggs Benedict, the place for the best luncheon hamburger - on the deck summers - and the best place for liver and onions, ribs and crab combo, beef stroganoff. If you go to Stanley's once, you'll return.  Ginny will be there to welcome you, a special customer, just like that.*

# Roquefort Dressing

| | |
|---|---|
| 1/2 | qt. mayonnaise |
| 1/3 | qt. buttermilk |
| 2 1/4 | oz. sour cream |
| 5 | oz. Roquefort cheese, grated |
| 1 | tsp. Coleman dry mustard |
| 1 | tsp. chopped dried onion |
| 1/4 | tsp. granulated garlic |
| 1 | tsp. black pepper |
| | salt to taste |
| 1/2 | tsp. Worcestershire Sauce |
| 1/2 | tsp. A-1 Sauce |

Blend all ingredients together.

*Makes 1 quart*

# Crab Omelette

| | |
|---|---|
| 1/4 | c. mushrooms, sliced |
| 1 | green onion, sliced |
| 1 | Tbsp. butter |
| 3 | eggs, whipped |
| 2 | oz. Alaskan crab meat |
| 1 | oz. Swiss cheese, grated |
| | Hollandaise Sauce |

Saute mushrooms and green onion in butter. Add the eggs. Flip the eggs over when they are softly cooked. Add crab on half of the omelette, cover with cheese. Bake in oven at 450° F. until cheese has melted. Fold omelette in half and cover with Hollandaise Sauce.

# Stanley's Omelette

2     oz. cooked ham, diced
2     Tbsp. butter, melted
3     eggs, whipped
2     strips mild green chili peppers
1     oz. Swiss cheese

In an omelette pan heat ham in butter. Add the eggs. Flip the eggs over when they are softly cooked. Add the mild green chili peppers, cover with Swiss cheese. Bake at 475° F. until cheese is melted, then fold onto a plate.

*Serves 1*

# Chicken Breast Supreme

1/4    c. flour
4      oz. chicken breast
1/4    c. butter, melted
1/3    c. white wine
1/3    c. fresh mushrooms, sliced
       dash tarragon
       dash pepper
       dash poultry seasoning

Flour chicken breast and cook in a saute pan on high heat until one side is slightly browned. Turn breast over, add melted butter, wine and mushrooms. Season to taste with tarragon, pepper and poultry seasoning. Simmer 20 to 30 minutes.

*Serves 1*

# Sauteed Liver

| | |
|---|---|
| 8 | oz. thinly sliced beef liver |
| 2 | Tbsp. oil |
| 1 | c. au jus |
| 1/3 | c. white wine |
| 1/3 | c. onion, chopped |
| 1/3 | c. mushrooms, chopped |
| 1 | tsp. garlic, minced |
| | pinch pepper |
| 1/2 | tsp. salt |

Cut the thinly sliced liver into 1/2" squares.  Saute liver in oil on high heat until both sides are slightly browned.  Add au jus, white wine, onion and mushrooms.  Season with garlic, pepper and salt. Simmer 20 to 30 minutes.

*Serves  1*

STEAK HOUSE
Harrah's Hotel and Casino
219 No. Center Street
Reno, NV 89520
(702) 786-3232
Hours: 5:00 p.m. - 12:00 a.m. Dinner, Daily
11:00 a.m. - 2:30 p.m. Lunch, Monday through Friday
Credit Cards: All major
Prices: Moderate to expensive
Reservations: Recommended
Specialties: Steaks and Continental Cuisine

*On the lower level of the Headliner Casino at the world-famous Harrah's, is the Steak House, a fine dining restaurant specializing in steaks and continental cuisine. The decor features fine wood paneling, rich leather upholstery and mirrored walls. You are served on linen, on bone china and in fine crystal. Tableside cooking is featured in this "Travel Holiday Magazine" award-winning restaurant. Evening entertainment adds to the continental atmosphere with classical guitar. Lunch is a fancy affair, also, featuring such enticing choices as escalope of veal or sole Veronique.*

233

# Poached Fillet of Petrale Sole

| | |
|---|---|
| 8 | 3-oz. fillet of petrale sole |
| | salt and pepper |
| 1 | head Chinese cabbage |
| 1 | c. white wine |
| 4 | Tbsp. butter |
| 2 | Tbsp. onions, chopped |
| 1 | c. long-grain rice, washed and drained |
| 2 | c. fish stock |
| | pinch turmeric |
| 1 | carrot, sliced thin |
| 1 | small turnip |
| 1 | c. heavy cream |
| 1/2 | bunch fresh tarragon, chopped |
| 1/2 | bunch fresh watercress, chopped |
| 1/2 | bunch spinach, chopped |
| 1 | Tbsp. butter |
| 1 | oz. golden caviar |
| 2 | doz. black beans, steamed until done |

Season fillets lightly with salt and pepper. Blanch cabbage for 10 seconds, cool and dry well. Wrap cabbage leaves around sole fillets. Place in poacher, pour in white wine and set aside. Meanwhile, in a saute pan, melt butter, add chopped onions and saute until transparent. Add the onions to the poacher. Add rice and stir until mixed. Add fish stock, turmeric and bring to a boil. Cover with a lid and simmer 25 minutes. Add carrots and cook about 2 minutes. Using a melon baller, cut 8 turnip balls, add turnip balls and continue cooking 2 minutes more. After fish is poached, remove and keep warm.

# P oached Fillet of Petrale Sole (Cont.)

Add cream and tarragon stems to poaching liquid and reduce to half. Season and strain. Add tarragon leaves, watercress and spinach to the strained sauce. Reheat and add butter. Pour sauce onto a heated plate, place 2 pieces of the poached sole on the plate, top with 1/8 oz. caviar on each piece. Put rice into small timbel, invert on plate, place 4 or 5 black beans on top of rice timbel for a garnish. Reheat carrots and turnip balls in butter. Place 1 turnip ball on top of carrot on each side of rice timbel.

*Serves 4*

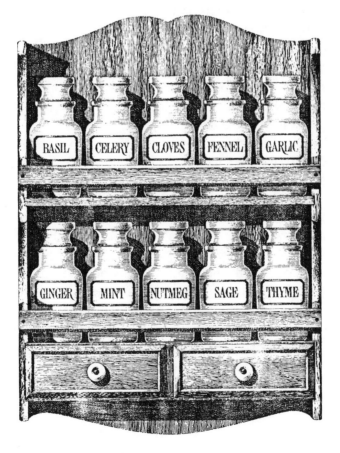

# Escargots Nicoise

| | |
|---|---|
| 3 | c. flour |
| 4 | large eggs |
| 1 | tsp. fresh oregano, chopped |
| 1 | tsp. fresh basil, chopped |
| 1 | tsp. fresh parsley, chopped |
| 1 | tsp. fresh thyme, chopped |
| 1 | tsp. fresh rosemary, chopped |
| 1 | Tbsp. oil |
| 1/2 | tsp. fresh garlic, chopped |
| 1/2 | tsp. fresh shallots, chopped |
| 2 | oz. butter |
| 2 | oz. white wine |
| 1/4 | medium tomato, blanched, seeded and chopped |
| 24 | snails, cut in half |
| 1/4 | tsp. anchovy paste |
| 1 | Tbsp. fresh parsley |
| | salt and black pepper |
| 3 | dashes Worcestershire Sauce |
| | sprigs of fresh rosemary |

Pour flour on working surface, shape into mound, make a well and add 2 eggs. Put remaining eggs and chopped herbs into blender, add olive oil and blend 5 seconds. Pour into well. Gradually work egg mixture into flour until eggs are absorbed. If sticky, add some more flour. Knead 8 to 10 minutes or until shiny. Set aside and cover with a towel. Allow to rest for 30 minutes. Roll out to a square sheet, 1/8" thick. Dust with flour. Roll loosely into a roll, cut to desired thickness.

## Escargots Nicoise (Cont.)

Boil in salted water for 3 minutes. Drain. Rinse under cold water. In a skillet, saute garlic and shallots in butter for 1 minute. Add white wine and tomatoes. Cook 1 minutes. Add snails, anchovy paste, parsley, seasonings and prepared pasta. Heat and toss. Garnish with rosemary.

*Serves 4*

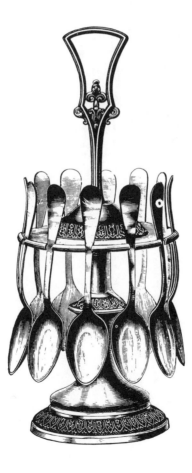

# STETSON'S

Del Webb's
High Sierra
Casino/Hotel Lake Tahoe

STETSON'S
Del Webb's High Sierra Casino
Highway 50 (P.O. Box C)
Stateline, NV
89449
(702)588-6211
Hours: 6:00 p.m. - 11:00 p.m.
Credit Cards: Visa, Mastercard, American Express, Diner's Club
Prices: Expensive
Reservations: Recommended
Specialties: Continental Cuisine

*The western motif at Stetson's centers on - what else - a cowboy hat, the famous Stetson. This chapeau played an important role in the colorful history of the Old West, and a display case shows off some of those Stetson styles that made cowboys look like cowboys. Booths are quiet and intimate, surrounded by beautiful silk flower arrangements. A single, long-stemmed rosebud softens every table and the service is charming. Catering to the most refined palate, Stetson's has a wide and varied selection of continental cuisine. Presentation of the food is artistically done with distinctive seasonings that do not overpower, but enhance each creation. An extensive wine list is available from the large selection of local California wineries to Chateau Lafite Rothchild.*

# Veal "High Sierra"

6       2-oz. pieces of veal, pounded thin
        salt
        white pepper
1/4     oz. clarified butter*
1/2     small shallot, minced
4       medium shiitake mushrooms
1/2     oz white wine
1/2     oz. demi-glace or brown sauce*
3       oz. butter
        chopped fresh parsley
        cooked fusilli noodles*

Season veal with salt and pepper to taste. Heat saute pan very hot, add clarified butter. Saute veal 30 seconds on each side. Remove from pan, pour out excess butter, add shallot. Saute quickly, add mushrooms and saute for a few seconds. In same pan, deglaze with wine; reduce by half. Add demi-glace or brown sauce. Add butter. Remove from heat and stir for a velvety sauce. Pour over veal. Garnish with chopped fresh parsley. Serve with buttered noodles.

*See glossary

*Serves 2*

# Petrale Sole "Veronique"

| | |
|---|---|
| 1 | 16 oz. petrale sole fillets (or any firm white fish) |
| | salt |
| | white pepper |
| | flour |
| 1 | Tbsp. clarified butter (see glossary) |
| 3 | Tbsp. whole butter |
| 3 | Tbsp. blanched almonds, sliced |
| 1/4 | c. Thompson seedless grapes |
| | juice of 1/2 a fresh lemon |
| 1 | tsp. white wine |
| | fresh parsley, chopped |

Season sole fillets with salt and pepper, then dust in flour. Heat saute pan, add clarified butter. Saute fillets 2 to 3 minutes on each side. Set fillets aside. Remove excess butter from pan. Add butter and almonds. Saute until golden brown, add grapes, lemon juice and white wine. Reduce until sauce thickens. Pour over fillets. Garnish with chopped fresh parsley.

*Serves 2*

LAKE    TAHOE

## SUNNYSIDE'S CHRIS CRAFT ROOM
1850 North Lake Blvd. (P.O. Box 5969)
Tahoe City, CA  95730
(916) 583-7200
Hours:  11:30 a.m.  Lunch
5:30 p.m.  Dinner
10:00 a.m.  Brunch, Saturday and Sunday
Credit Cards:  American Express, MasterCard, Visa
Prices:  Moderate
Reservations:  Suggested
Specialties:  Seafood

*Sunnyside resort, a popular spot for over 80 years on the West Shore of Lake Tahoe, has undergone a multi-bucks expansion and renovation . . . and still serves its famous deep-fried zucchini.  Sunnyside's famous appetizer brings us back again and again, and those who've tasted it will be thankful they can still order it.*

*The Old Tahoe charm and tradition are once again a part of Sunnyside - you'll love it.  As folks say, who have returned after 20 years or more, "Why, it's just like I remember it."  In fact, the renovation brought back the real feel of the good-old-days ambience of a historical site on the shores of Tahoe.  Reachable by tarmac hiway or water biway (you can tie your boat up at Sunnyside's marina), Sunnyside is a captivating stop.  Driving or boating the Tahoe scene, don't miss Sunnyside. The Chris Craft Room is the main dining salon, but you can also dine in the Lake Room overlooking the marina, or the Emerald Room, on the Emerald Bay side of the resort.*

243

# Chinese Chicken Salad

| | |
|---|---|
| 1/2 | head butter lettuce, chopped (set aside the outer leaves) |
| 6 | oz. linguine, cooked |
| 4 | oz. chicken strips |
| 10 | snow peas, julienned |
| 1/4 | c. carrots, julienned |
| 1/4 | c. red bell pepper, julienned |
| 2 | green onions, julienned |
| 2 | Tbsp. sesame mayonnaise (recipe follows) |

In a glass bowl, arrange the outer leaves of the butter lettuce  Add the chopped butter lettuce, linguine, chicken strips and julienned vegetables.  Top with Sesame mayonnaise.

*Serves 2*

# Sesame Mayonnaise

| | |
|---|---|
| 1 | c. Mayonnaise |
| 1 | Tbsp. sesame oil* |
| 1/4 | tsp. hot chili oil* |
| 1 | Tbsp. soy sauce |
| 1 | Tbsp. green onions, minced |
| 1 | Tbsp. toasted sesame seeds |

Blend all ingredients together.

*Available in Oriental markets

*Yields 1 1/4 cups*

# Fettucine Pescatoro

| | |
|---|---|
| 1 | c. white wine |
| | splash lemon juice |
| 1/2 | tsp. garlic, minced |
| 1 | Tbsp. butter |
| 2 | whole prawns, peeled and deveined |
| 3 | oz. scallops |
| 2 | oz. mussels |
| 2 | oz. clams |
| 1 | c. heavy cream |
| 2 1/2 | oz. bay shrimp |
| 6 | oz. fettucine, cooked |
| 3 | oz. Parmesan cheese, shredded |
| | salt and pepper to taste |
| | lemon wedges |
| | parsley, chopped |
| | Parmesan cheese, ground |

Heat wine, lemon juice and garlic in butter. Turn heat to high and add prawns, scallops, mussels and clams, being careful not to overcook scallops or prawns. Add cream and simmer for 1 minute. Add bay shrimp, pasta, shredded Parmesan, salt and pepper to taste. Garnish with lemon wedges and top with chopped parsley and grated Parmesan.

*Serves 2*

# Macadamia Nut Scallops

| 2 | lbs. bay scallops (30 - 40 count), thawed |
| | flour |
| 2 | eggs |
| 2 | c. milk |

*Breading:*

| 1/4 | c. chopped macadamia nuts |
| 1/4 | c. bread crumbs |
| 1/4 | c. Parmesan cheese, grated |

*Sauce:*

| 1 | c. white wine |
| 1 | Tbsp. shallots |
| 1/2 | tsp. garlic |
| 1 | c. heavy cream |
| 1 | lb. butter, cut in cubes |
| | lemon juice |
| 1 | large red bell pepper |

Dredge scallops in flour, egg wash (see glossary) and macadamia nut breading. Scallops may be sauteed in a pan with 1 Tablespoon butter, or deep fried. Cook to a golden brown. Remove the scallops to a warm plate. In the saute pan, add wine and reduce. Add shallots, garlic and cream. Reduce again. Add butter slowly. Add lemon juice to taste. Roast one large red bell pepper in oven. Remove skin and seeds. Puree the pepper in a blender or a food processor. Add the pureed pepper to the sauce. Serve sauce on the side for dipping.

*Serves 4*

**LODGE / CASINO**
**CRYSTAL BAY, NEV**

TAHOE BILTMORE
Number 5 Highway 28 (P.O. Box 115)
Crystal Bay, NV 89402
(702) 831-0660
Hours: Twenty-four hours a day, seven days a week
9:00 a.m. - 3:00 p.m. Sunday brunch
5:00 p.m. - 10:00 p.m. Buffet, Friday and Saturday
11:00 a.m. - 3:00 p.m. Lunch buffet, daily
Credit Cards: All major
Prices: Inexpensive
Reservations: Not required
Specialties: Good American food

*The forest green, the glass and brass - it's a whole new look at the Tahoe Biltmore's large dining room. With new chefs, new menu and the same old friendly service, the Biltmore Restaurant has become one of the North Shore's favorite spots for consistently good American meals. The service is smooth and quick, and the buffets are piled high with beautifully presented dishes to tempt you. It's difficult to pass any of them up. The Biltmore is a place where you'll see friends, and a restaurant that you'll return to. After dinner you can also enjoy the live music in the Savoy Lounge next door. The entire casino thrives on a friendly, warm atmosphere - you'll feel at home here.*

# Korean Chicken Salad

| | |
|---|---|
| 2 | chicken breasts, skinned and boned |
| 1 | oz. corn oil |
| 1 | oz. butter |
| 2 | stalks celery, julienned |
| 12 | water chestnuts |
| 1/3 | c. bamboo shoots |
| 1 - 2 | Tbsp. sesame seeds, toasted |
| 1/4 | c. fresh bean sprouts |

*Dressing:*

| | |
|---|---|
| 1/4 | c. salad oil |
| 1/4 | c. soy sauce |
| 2 | tsp. dry sherry wine |
| 1 - 2 | Tbsp. brown sugar |

Saute chicken in oil and butter until done. After cooling, cut the chicken into thin strips and place in a large bowl. Add the celery, water chestnuts, bamboo shoots, toasted sesame seeds and bean sprouts. Prepare the dressing and pour over entire mixture. Let marinate for at least 12 hours. Serve cold on a bed of lettuce.

*Serves 2*

**TAHOE GRILLE**
700 North Lake Blvd.
Tahoe City, CA  95730
(916) 583-4053
Hours:  5:00 p.m. - 10:00 p.m.  Seven nights a week
Credit Cards:  American Express, Visa, Mastercard
Prices:  Moderate
Reservations:  Large groups only
Specialties:  Baby Back Ribs

*In the historical setting of the Roundhouse Mall in Tahoe City, Tahoe Grille flourishes, gaining on itself every day as the word gets around . . . the Grille is a great place to eat.  Owner Scott Litteral likes light cooking and uses oakwood-smoked and mesquite-grilled methods for his mixed grill specialties. Old Tahoe in atmosphere, Tahoe Grille shows off its excellent collection of old-time Basin photos, always a delight to diners.  Your choices for dinner will range from California lamb chops, linquica and Delta catfish to fetucine Alfredo or sandwiches. Top it all of with a piece of apple pie a la mode and your evening will be completely satisfying.*

# Creole Sauce for Sauteed Catfish

| | |
|---|---|
| 1 | c. onion, diced |
| 1 | c. celery, diced |
| 1 | c. bell pepper, diced |
| 1 | tsp. sweet basil |
| 1 | tsp. garlic, minced |
| 1 | tsp. Creole spices |
| 4 | oz. butter |
| 4 | c. tomatoes, stewed |
| 1 | c. tomato sauce |
| 1 | c. water |

Saute vegetables, garlic and spices in butter.  Add stewed tomatoes, tomato sauce and water.  Cook until vegetables are tender and serve with sauteed catfish.

*Serves 4 to 6*

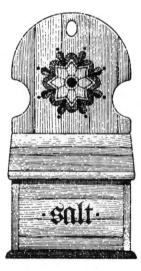

# Swiss Cuisine

**TAHOE HOUSE**

**1/2 mile south of Tahoe City "Y" on Hwy. 89 (P. O. Drawer S)**

**Tahoe City, CA  95730**

**(916) 583-1377**

**Hours:  5:00 p.m. to closing**

**Credit Cards:  Mastercard, Visa, American Express**

**Prices:  Moderate**

**Reservations:  Suggested**

**Specialties:  Swiss Cuisine**

*What better place to enjoy Swiss cuisine than in the Alpine splendour of Lake Tahoe in the warm and comforable knotty-pine interior of Tahoe House.  The lounge sports a wonderfully large rock fireplace, the kind you need in a mountain setting - good for both apres ski evenings or chilly summer nights.  Owner and chef, Peter Vogt, does right by his customers always, with veal specialties, steaks, seafood specials and homemade breads and pastries.  Mmmmm, those desserts of Peter's could just as well be made in heaven.  Even if you NEVER eat dessert, I bet at Tahoe House you will.*

# Spinach Salad

6       slices of bacon, cut in strips
1/2     c. salad oil
1/2     fresh lemon, juiced
1/4     tsp. garlic, chopped
1/2     tsp. mustard
1/2     fresh orange, juiced
1/3     c. red wine vinegar
        salt & pepper to taste
        dash Worchestershire and hot sauce
        brandy (optional)
2       large bunches spinach, washed and stems trimmed

Pan fry bacon until crisp. Drain fat and add remaining ingredients except the spinach, heating thoroughly. Flame with brandy if desired. Pour the hot dressing over the spinach and let the salad wilt for 2 minutes. Mix well and serve.

*Serves 4*

# Tahoe House Golden Honey Dressing

1       16 oz. jar mayonnaise
1/4     c. red wine vinegar
1       Tbsp. prepared mustard
1       c. honey
1       Tbsp. parsley flakes
        salt and pepper to taste

### Tahoe House Golden Honey Dressing (Cont.)

Put mayonnaise in mixing bowl, add vinegar and mustard. Add honey while whipping continually. Add parsley and season to taste with salt and pepper.

(This dressing will separate when stored over an extended period of time. This does not affect the product, just whip or shake well before serving.) Sunflower seeds or raisins add that special touch to Golden Honey Dressing.

*Yields 3 1/4 cups*

# Swiss Cheese Fondue

| | |
|---|---|
| 1/2 | clove garlic |
| 1 1/2 | pt. chablis |
| 1 | bay leaf |
| | Nutmeg, salt, pepper and paprika to taste |
| 8 | oz. imported Swiss cheese, grated |
| 8 | oz. Gruyere cheese, grated |
| 8 | oz. Appenzeller cheese, grated |
| 1 | oz. Kirschwasser |
| 2 | tsp. cornstarch |

Rub the inside of the fondue pot with garlic. Add wine, bay leaf and seasoning and bring to a boil. Slowly add the grated cheeses to the wine. Stir until all the cheese is dissolved. Mix Kirschwasser and cornstarch together. Add to the boiling fondue and mix well. Serve the fondue boiling hot with cubes of French bread.

*Serves 4*

# Quiche Lorraine

| | |
|---|---|
| 2 | Tbsp. chives, freeze dried or fresh |
| 2 | slices of diced ham or cooked bacon |
| 1 | pre-made pie shell |
| 1/3 | lb. Emmenthaler or other imported Swiss cheese, grated |
| 1/3 | lb. Raclette cheese, grated |
| 1/3 | lb. domestic Swiss cheese, grated |
| 3 | eggs, beaten |
| 1 1/2 | c. half and half |
| | salt, pepper and nutmeg to taste |

Arrange chives and ham or bacon in bottom pie shell. Cover with
the grated cheeses. In a bowl mix together eggs, half and half and
seasonings. Pour over the cheeses. Bake at 375° F. for approximately 20 to 25 minutes.

*Serves 8*

# Forellon Blau (Trout Blue)

1 1/2    gallon water
2        Tbsp. salt
1/2      Tbsp. whole peppercorns
1/4      c. white vinegar
1        c. sliced carrot, onion and celery (combined)
1        bay leaf
1        clove
4        fresh trout, cleaned

Combine first 7 ingredients ingredients and bring to boil. Reduce heat to simmer, add trout and let simmer for 10-12 minutes. Fish is done when back breaks and bone is visible. Remove fish and serve.

Note: When washing and cleaning fish, be careful to preserve natural slime on trout - without this, and the fact that the trout are fresh, the skin will not turn blue.

*Serves 4*

# Rahmschnitzel Zuercherart

| | |
|---|---|
| 1/3 | c. flour |
| | salt and pepper to taste |
| 8 | thin slices of veal or lean boneless pork loin |
| 2 | Tbsp. oil |
| 1 | Tbsp. shallots or onions, finely chopped |
| 1/2 | lb. fresh mushrooms, thinly sliced |
| 1/2 | c. white wine |
| 1 1/2 | c. whipping cream |
| 1 | tsp. chicken base |
| | salt, pepper and paprika to taste |

Mix flour, salt and pepper. Dredge meat in flour mixture and pan fry in hot oil until brown on both sides. Remove meat from pan and add shallots or onions. Saute. Add mushrooms and wine. Add cream, chicken base and seasonings. Simmer the sauce for 2 minutes. Return the meat to the pan and simmer for approximately 2 minutes. Serve with rice or noodles.

*Serves 4*

# Strawberries Romanoff

| | |
|---|---|
| 1 | basket strawberries, washed and cut in half |
| 1 | c. whipped cream |
| | sugar, Kirschwasser, Cointreau and strawberry liquor to taste |
| 1/3 | tsp. grated orange rind |
| 4 | scoops vanilla ice cream |

## Strawberries Romanoff (Cont.)

Place all ingredients except ice cream in bowl and mix well. Put a small scoop of vanilla ice cream in a wine glass and spoon straw-berry mixture over ice cream.

*Serves 4*

# Zabaglione with Fresh Fruit

| | |
|---|---|
| 1/2 | c. sugar |
| 6 | egg yolks |
| | orange and lemon peel, grated |
| 1/2 | c. white wine |
| 1 | oz. Cointreau |
| 1 | tsp. vanilla extract |
| 4 | scoops vanilla ice cream |
| | fresh strawberries or raspberries |

Beat sugar and egg yolks until mixture forms a "ribbon". Flavor with orange and lemon peel. Add white wine, Cointreau and vanilla. Cook mixture in double boiler over very low heat, whisk-ing it vigorously until it becomes frothy stiff. Scoop ice cream into large wine glasses, add fruit and top with the hot Zabaglione sauce.

*Serves 4*

# Linzer Torte

| | |
|---|---|
| 7 | oz. flour |
| 3 | oz. sugar |
| 5 | oz. butter |
| 5 1/2 | oz. grated almonds |
| 1 | egg |
| 1 | tsp. baking powder |
| 1/2 | tsp. cinnamon |
| 1/4 | tsp. ground cloves |
| 8 | oz. raspberry marmalade |

Form a ring with the flour. Add all the other ingredients except the marmalade and mix well, insuring that all the ingredients are well combined. Let rest for 30 minutes and roll into 1/4 inch thickness. Use a 9" cake pan to cut out a circle in the dough. Place the dough in the pan and cover with raspberry marmalade. Use remaining dough to decorate the top and brush pastry with egg wash (see glossary). Bake 25-30 minutes in a 375° F. oven.

*Serves 6-8*

# The Terrace

AT EDGEWOOD

**THE TERRACE LAKESIDE RESTAURANT**
Highway 50 at Lake Parkway (P.O. Box 5400)
Stateline, NV  89449
(702) 588-2787
Hours:  11:00 a.m. - 2:00 p.m.  Lunch, daily, summers only
6:00 p.m. - until closing  Dinner, daily
10:00 a.m. - 2:00 p.m.  Sunday brunch, summer only
Credit Cards:  American Express, Visa
Prices:  Moderate
Reservations:  Recommended
Specialties:  Steak and Seafood

*At the most famous and prestigious golf course at Lake Tahoe sits a most famous and prestigious restaurant - The Terrace at Edgewood. Whether you're a golfer or not, The Terrace is a great dining-out idea, for the food is exceptional and the views of Lake Tahoe unprecedented. The Terrace is simply warm and inviting, casual yet elegant, intimate yet expansive. The menu offers veal, calamari, lobster, salmon, swordfish, duckling, lamb, filet mignon and an unusual quail and scampi combination. Candlelight dining, private parties, professional service, friendly atmosphere - The Terrace at Edgewood Golf Course is a lovely place to dine.*

# Fresh Mushroom Bouchee

| | |
|---|---|
| 1 | pkg. puff pastry |
| 4 | oz. chanterelles |
| 4 | oz. cepes |
| 4 | oz. shiitake mushrooms |
| 2 | Tbsp. butter |
| 1 | Tbsp. shallots, minced |
| 1/2 | c. Madeira |
| 1/2 | c. heavy whipping cream |
| 1/2 | c. veal stock or brown sauce (see glossary) |
| | fresh parsley for garnish |

Cut pastry into 4 pieces, use eggwash (see glossary) and bake at 400° F. until golden brown. Saute mushrooms in butter with shallots. Add Madeira and reduce by half. Add cream and veal stock or brown sauce, reduce by half again. Cut pastry into 2 pieces, place mushrooms on top of 1 piece and place the other piece on top of mushrooms. Garnish with parsley.

*Serves 4*

# Fresh Stuffed Quail with Redcurrant Sauce

| | |
|---|---|
| 4 | oz. Jack Cheese |
| 4 | oz. almonds, finely chopped |
| 1 | red apple, finely chopped |
| 1 | tsp. allspice |
| 1 | egg |
| 4 | quail |
| 3 | oz. olive oil |
| | fine bread crumbs |
| | redcurrant jelly |
| 2 | oz. blackberry brandy |
| 1 | oz. amaretto |
| 4 | oz. demi-glace or brown sauce (see glossary) |

Crumble cheese in small bits and mix with almonds and apple in mixing bowl.  Add allspice and egg and blend thoroughly with spoon.  Using pastry bag or fingers, fill quail until plump.  In large pan heat olive oil.  Coat quail in fine bread crumbs.  Place in pan. Turn quail when edges are golden brown and place in 350° F. oven for 8-10 minutes.  In saute pan, place jelly, brandy, amaretto and demi-glace, heat over medium flame and whisk until blended. Lower heat and simmer until sauce thickens

*Serves 4*

# Cherries Edgewood

| | |
|---|---|
| 1 | 8-oz. can bing cherries |
| 1/4 | c. Kirshwasser |
| | pinch nutmeg |
| | pinch cinnamon |
| 1/2 | orange rind, grated |
| | orange juice, squeezed |
| 1/2 | lemon rind, grated |
| | lemon juice, squeezed |
| 1/4 | c. brown sugar |
| 2 | Tbsp. cornstarch dissolved in 1/2 c. water |

Place all ingredients in a saute pan except cornstarch solution. As it comes to the boil slowly add cornstarch until thickened and Serve over ice cream.

*Yields 1 1/2 cups*

# A CATERED AFFAIR 🐖
## Take It Away!

**THERESA MAY DUGGAN'S A CATERED AFFAIR**

P.O. Box 290

Tahoe Vista, CA 95732

(916) 546-3074

Parties for two or 600, catered for breakfast. brunch, lunch, cocktails. dinner or picnics

Credit Cards: None

Prices: Inexpensive to expensive, depending on customer's desire

Reservations: At least forty-eight hours notice

Specialties: California Mixed Grill

*Theresa May Duggan makes a "special affair" no matter the size or ticket price of the affair she is catering. Although best known for her California Mixed Grill, Cordon Bleu-trained Duggan will do anything a host or hostess wants in the culinary line - all Japanese, with sushi, sashimi and yakitori? All Southwest - with the authentic dishes researched and tested before the big event? Tres fancy or downright informal? A Catered Affair prides itself on its professionalism, no matter the occasion. The food is exquisitely prepared and served on time to raves of "Where did you get this stuff?" And your house is cleaned within an inch of its life before they leave. A Catered Affair has raised the standards of catering among the casual lifestyles of the mountains and it's a blessing to any classy hostess.*

# Hot Crab Dip

| | |
|---|---|
| 4 | oz. Jack cheese, grated |
| 4 | oz. cream cheese |
| 1 | egg |
| | dash Tabasco |
| 1 | Tbsp. horseradish |
| | fresh parsley, chopped |
| | dash Worcestershire Sauce |
| 1/4 | c. onion, pureed |
| 4 | oz. Dungeness or snow crab |

Cream together Jack and cream cheese with egg. Add all other ingredients and put in souffle or other ovenproof dish. Heat at 375° F. until bubbly. Serve with crackers, celery sticks or toast.

*Yields 2 cups*

# Vinaigrette

| | |
|---|---|
| 1 | 12-oz. jar Dijon mustard |
| 1 1/2 | c. olive oil |
| 2 1/2 | c. salad oil |
| 1 | c. vinegar |
| 2 | Tbsp. parsley, chopped |
| 1 | Tbsp. tarragon |
| 1 | Tbsp. thyme |
| 1/2 | Tbsp. oregano |
| 1/2 | Tbsp. basil |
| 1/2 | medium yellow onion, pureed |
| 2 | small cloves garlic |
| 1 | tsp. Pernod |
| | |
| 1 | tsp. brandy |
| 1 | Tbsp. white wine |
| | salt and pepper to taste |

In a food processor add mustard and slowly drip in the oils until thick and creamy. Gradually add vinegar. Add herbs, onion, garlic, Pernod, brandy and wine. Process only a minute or so. Refrigerate.

*Yields 7 cups*

# Bleu Cheese Mold Elizabeth

| | |
|---|---|
| 4 | oz. whipping cream |
| 4 | oz. bleu cheese |
| 4 | oz. cream cheese |
| 4 | oz. butter |
| 1 | Tbsp. fresh parsley, chopped |
| 1 | Tbsp. fresh tarragon, chopped |
| 1 | Tbsp. fresh chives, chopped |

Whip cream and set aside. Cream together next 3 ingredients, add herbs, fold in whipped cream. Either put in ring mold or pipe out of pastry bag. Can also be formed into cheese ball and rolled in chopped parsley or walnuts.

*Yields 2 cups*

# Mmmmmmmm Cheesecake

*Crust:*

| | |
|---|---|
| 4 | oz. butter |
| 1 1/2 | c. graham crackers |
| 1/4 | c. sugar |
| | cinnamon to taste |

Melt butter, add to graham crackers, sugar and cinnamon. Pack tightly in 10-inch cheesecake pan and bake at 375° F. for 6 minutes or until set. Let cool.

## Mmmmmmmm Cheesecake (cont.)

*Filling:*

| | |
|---|---|
| 24 | oz. cream cheese |
| 1 | c. sugar |
| 4 | eggs |
| 1 | Tbsp. vanilla |

Cream together cream cheese and sugar, add eggs one at a time, beating after each addition. Add vanilla. Bake at 375° F. for 32 minutes. Let cool 10 minutes.

*Topping:*

| | |
|---|---|
| 12 | oz. sour cream |
| 1/4 | c. sugar |
| | vanilla to taste |

Cream together all ingredients, spread on top of cheesecake and bake 6 minutes at 400° F. Let cool 24 hours.

*Serves 12 to 16*

# Theresa's Nifty Little Tricks

*Onion Puree*

| | |
|---|---|
| 2 | medium yellow onions, roughly chopped |
| 1/4 | c. white wine |

In a food processor add onion and wine. Run Cuisinart until a fine puree is produced. This onion puree will last for about 4 days and is easy to add to recipes calling for onion.

*Garlic Puree*

2      whole flowers garlic, peeled
1/4    c. olive oil

In a food processor add garlic, running machine as olive oil is added to create a fine paste. This garlic puree will last 2 to 3 weeks in a tightly-covered jar in the refrigerator. Use 1/2 tsp. to equal 1 clove garlic.

# TIMBER HOUSE

# Lakeside Inn
## —— & CASINO ——

**TIMBER HOUSE RESTAURANT**
Lakeside Inn and Casino
Highway 50 at Kingsbury Grade (P.O. Box 5640)
Stateline, NV   89449
(702) 588-7777
Hours:  Twenty-four hours a day, seven days a week, breakfast and lunch
500 p.m. - 11:00 p.m.  Dinner
Credit Cards:  All major
Prices:  Moderate
Reservations:  Not required
Specialties:  Continental

*Lakeside Casino's Timber House Restaurant combines a country inn atmosphere
with a wonderfully varied traditional menu. Situated as it is on Kingsbury Grade,
Timber House offers spectacular vistas - Lake Tahoe, the mountains, the forests,
the unbelievable blue of Tahoe skies.  It's an inspiring place to eat because of the
views . . . and the food.  The chocolate cheesecake is outrageously wonderful,
enough to make you think you've died and gone to heaven. It is possibly the best
west of the Hudson.*

# Linguine Aglio E. Olio Saetini

| | |
|---|---|
| 1 | Tbsp. parsley, chopped |
| 1/4 | tsp. red peppers, crushed |
| 5 | oz. oil |
| 1 | lb. linguine, cooked al dente |
| 1 | oz. Parmesan cheese, grated |

Saute parsley and peppers in oil until lightly cooked. Toss linguine lightly in sauce, add Parmesan cheese and serve.

*Serves 2*

# Clams Arreganata

| | |
|---|---|
| 6 | clams |
| 1 | oz. Parmesan cheese, grated |
| 1/3 | c. seasoned bread crumbs |
| 1 | Tbsp. lemon juice |
| 1 | Tbsp. oil |
| | lemon slices to garnish |
| | parsley sprigs to garnish |

Wash clams thoroughly and open. Discard 1 shell and loosen clams from other shell. Mix Parmesan, bread crumbs, lemon juice and oil together. Place equal amount of this mixture on each clam. Place clams on sizzler and bake in oven until lightly browned. Serve on garnished plate.

*Serves 2*

# Sauerbraten Beef

| | |
|---|---|
| 3 | pts. cold water |
| | c. Burgandy wine |
| 4 | oz. carrots, sliced thin |
| 1 | cloves garlic, chopped |
| 1 | Tbsp. pickling spice |
| 1 | c. red wine vinegar |
| 1/1 | lb. onions, sliced thin |
| 1 | rib of celery, sliced thin |
| 1/2 | oz. brown sugar |
| | juniper berries |
| 6 | lbs. bottom round of beef |
| 1/4 | c. oil |
| 1/4 | lb. ginger snaps, crushed |

Place first 10 ingredients into a ceramic casserole and stir well. Place meat in casserole and cover. Marinate in refrigerator 3 days, remove the meat and wipe it dry. In a frying pan brown the meat in hot oil. Place browned meat in a large pot, add marinade and cover. Bring to a boil and simmer for 2 hours. When meat is done, transfer it to a pan and cover with a damp cloth to keep warm. Whip crushed ginger snaps into marinade liquid and stir until smooth and thickened. Cut meat cross-grained and serve with marinade sauce.

*Serves 12*

# Cardinale Chocolate Cheesecake

| | |
|---|---|
| 1 | 6-oz. pkg. (1 c.) Nestle's Semi-Sweet Chocolate Morsels |
| 1/2 | c. sugar |
| 1 1/4 | c. graham cracker crumbs |
| 2 | Tbsp. sugar |
| 1/4 | c. melted butter |
| 2 | 8-oz. packages cream cheese, softened |
| 3/4 | c. sugar |
| 1/2 | c. sour cream |
| 1 | tsp. vanilla |
| 4 | eggs |

Preheat oven to 325° F. Over a double boiler combine chocolate chips and sugar. Heat until morsels and sugar melt and mixture is smooth. Remove from heat and set aside. Combine graham cracker crumbs with 2 tablespoons sugar and melted butter. Mix well and pat firmly into 1-9" spring form pan, a 1/2" up the side. Set aside. In a large bowl beat cream cheese until light and creamy. Gradually beat in 3/4 cup sugar, sour cream, vanilla and add eggs 1 at a time, beating well after each addition. Divide batter in half and stir melted chocolate mixture into first half. Pour into prepared crust and cover with plain batter. With a knife, swirl plain batter with chocolate batter to marbelize. Bake at 325° F. for 50 minutes. Cool at room temperature. Refrigerate until ready to serve.

Makes one 9" cake.

*Serves 8*

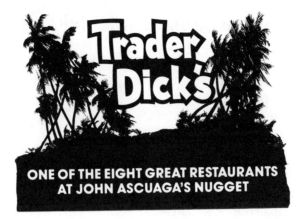

ONE OF THE EIGHT GREAT RESTAURANTS
AT JOHN ASCUAGA'S NUGGET

**TRADER DICK'S**
John Ascuaga's Nugget
1100 Nugget Ave. (P.O. Box 797)
Sparks, NV 89432
(702) 356-3300
Hours: 11:00 a.m. - 2:00 p.m. Lunch
5:00 p.m. - 11:00 p.m. Dinner
Credit Cards: Visa, Mastercard, American Express
Prices: Moderate
Reservations: Recommended
Specialties: Polynesian and Traditional

*Trader Dick's is a tradition in a town known for its fine casino dining. Originally located across the street from John Ascuaga's Nugget, Trader Dick's was moved in 1973 to its current location in the popular casino. Having just undergone a thorough revamping - you won't know the place if you haven't been there for a while - Trader's emerged more lovely than ever, an enchanting place of tropical greenery, a 6,000-gallon, 45-foot aquarium filled with exotic tropical fish, and the same wonderfully-prepared, elegantly-served Polynesian fare. But if you are the traditional gastronome, Trader Dick's still offers prime rib, lobster and steak.*

# Asparagus with Chicken

| | |
|---|---|
| 1/2 | oz. peanut oil |
| | few drops sesame oil |
| 1/2 | tsp. salt |
| | dash of garlic powder |
| | dash of ground ginger |
| 4 | oz. chicken breast, chopped |
| 1 | oz. water chestnuts, sliced |
| 1 | oz. mushrooms, sliced |
| 4 | oz. fresh asparagus, cut |
| 1 | tsp. wild plum sauce |
| 6 | oz. chicken broth |
| 2 | tsp. cornstarch |

Heat wok to high, add peanut oil and sesame oil, salt, garlic powder, ginger, chicken, all the vegetables and wild plum sauce. Saute. Add chicken broth and cook for about 1 minute. Add cornstarch to thicken. Bring to boil. Simmer for 2 minutes.

*Serves 4*

# Shrimp and Lobster Cantonese

| | |
|---|---|
| 1 | oz. peanut oil |
| 1/2 | tsp. salt |
| 1/2 | tsp. black bean sauce* |
| 4 | oz. jumbo fillet of prawn |
| 3 | oz. lobster fillet |
| 1 | oz. ham, diced |
| 2 | Tbsp. sherry |
| 8 | oz. chicken broth |
| 6 | water chestnuts, sliced |
| 3 | drops of sesame oil* |
| | pinch white pepper |
| 1 | tsp. cornstarch |
| 1 | fresh egg |
| 1 | tsp. green onion, chopped |

Assemble all ingredients together on the side. Place a wok on high. Add peanut oil, salt and black bean sauce. Stir them with a spatula until a strong aroma emerges. Add the prawn, lobster and ham to the wok and saute a few minutes. Add the sherry and chicken broth. Cover and cook for 2 minutes. Lift the cover and add water chestnuts, sesame oil and white pepper. Add cornstarch to desired thickness. Last, beat the egg into the sauce. Cook for 1/2 minute. Garnish with chopped green onion.

*Available in Oriental markets

*Serves 4*

# Steak Kew

| | |
|---|---|
| 1/2 | oz. peanut oil |
| 1 | lb. Tenderloin steak |
| 1 | tsp. sherry |
| 2 | c. Combination of mushrooms, water chestnuts, bamboo shoots, carrots, onions, baby corn, snow peas |
| 6 | oz. chicken broth |
| 3 | drops of sesame oil* |
| 1 | tsp. oyster sauce* |
| 1/2 | tsp. salt |
| | dash of garlic powder |
| | dash of powdered ginger |
| 2 | tsp. cornstarch |

Preheat wok to medium-high heat, add peanut oil and Tenderloin.  Brown both sides.  Add sherry and vegetables, mix and quickly saute.  Add chicken broth, cover wok and cook for 2 minutes.  Add sesame oil, oyster sauce, salt and garlic powder with ginger.  Add cornstarch to desired thickness.

*Available in Oriental markets

*Serves 4*

276

**THE VINTAGE**
Eldorado Casino
345 No. Virginia Street
Reno, NV  89505
(703) 786-5700
Hours:  5:00 p.m. - 11:00 p.m.
Credit Cards:  All major
Prices:  Moderate
Reservations:  Accepted
Specialties:  Steak and Seafood

*The Vintage in the Eldorado Hotel Casino features steak and seafood specialties for dinner with complementary West Coast wine tastings every evening. The menu includes at least one daily special, along with the specialties of the house which are Veal Florentine, Steak Diane a la Vintage and Veal Oscar. The Bananas Flambe for dessert is fancy and delicious - a fantastic way to end a meal.*

# Mesquite Grilled Lamb Chops

| | |
|---|---|
| 2 | Tbsp. balsamic vinegar |
| 1 | c. olive oil |
| 1 | medium garlic clove, minced |
| 1 | Tbsp. fresh rosemary, finely chopped |
| 8 | rib lamb chops, each about 3/4" thick |
| | mesquite chips |
| | charcoal |

*Rosemary Sauce:*

| | |
|---|---|
| 1/2 | tsp. shallots, minced |
| 1 1/2 | tsp. butter |
| 2 | oz. white wine |
| 2 | Tbsp. fresh rosemary, chopped |
| 1/2 | tsp. sugar |
| 1 | c. chicken stock |

Combine balsamic vinegar, olive oil, garlic and rosemary. Marinate the lamb chops with the vinegar mixture, overnight in the refrigerator, turning the meat once or twice. Remove the meat from the marinade and pat lightly with paper towels. Soak mesquite chips in water while charcoal is burning to white coals. Add the chips to the coals and wait about 5 minutes. Grill the chops about 4 minutes on each side or until desired doneness. Meanwhile, in a small saute pan, place the remaining ingredients for the sauce. Bring to a boil and then simmer for 10 minutes. Place the grilled lamb chops on warmed serving platter and serve the rosemary sauce on the side.

*Serves 4*

# Prosciutto Wrapped Prawns

12      slices prosciutto ham, thinly sliced
12      medium basil leaves
12      jumbo shrimp, peeled and deveined
        olive oil
*Sauce:*
2       c. chicken stock
7       fresh basil leaves, chopped
1       Tbsp. butter

Top a slice of prosciutto with a basil leaf. Starting at one end, roll the prosciutto and basil around the middle of the shrimp. Proceed to roll all 12 shrimp in this fashion. Thread 3 prawns on each of 4 skewers. Dip each skewer in olive oil and broil 6" from heat. Grill approximately 3 minutes on each side. For the sauce, place the stock and basil in a pan over medium high heat. Reduce the liquid in the pan by one half. Add the butter and stir until melted. Remove the prawns from skewers and arrange on plates. Serve sauce over the top.

*Serves 4*

# Steak Diane

| | |
|---|---|
| 2 | Tbsp. butter |
| 8 | 3-oz. fillet mignon |
| 1/2 | lb. fresh mushrooms, sliced |
| 2 | Tbsp. shallots, minced |
| 4 | oz. demi-glace (See Glossary) |
| 3 | Tbsp. heavy cream |
| 2 | Tbsp. Dijon mustard |
| 2 | Tbsp. brandy |
| | salt and pepper to taste |
| | dash of Worcestershire Sauce |

Heat butter in saute pan until very hot. Add fillets and cook rare. Add the mushrooms and shallots and cook 2 minutes. Add demi-glace, cream, mustard, brandy, salt, pepper and Worcestershire. Bring to a quick boil and immediately remove from heat. Serve at once. The entire cooking time is only about 5 to 7 minutes, depending on desired doneness of the meat.

*Serves 4*

# Bananas Flambe

| | |
|---|---|
| 2 | oz. butter |
| | peel of 1 lemon, grated |
| 4 | bananas, sliced lengthwise |
| 1 | oz. almonds, toasted and slivered |
| | juice of 1 lemon |
| | juice of 1 orange |
| 2 | oz. banana liqueur |
| 2 | oz. Grand Marnier |
| 3 | oz. brown sugar |
| | vanilla ice cream |

Heat butter in non-stick pan until very hot. Add lemon peel, stir for 3 seconds. Add bananas, almonds, fruit juices, liqueurs and brown sugar. Heat very gently. Ignite the contents of the pan and hold away from heat. When flame dies serve over vanilla ice cream.

*Serves 4*

# *The* *Wildflower* *Café*

**THE WILDFLOWER CAFE**

869 Tahoe Blvd. (P. O. Box 7473)

Incline Village, NV 89450

(702) 831-8072

Hours: 7 a.m. - 2:30 p.m. Monday - Saturday

8 a.m. - 2 p.m. Sunday

Credit Cards: American Express, Mastercard, Visa

Prices: Inexpensive to moderate

Reservations: Not required

Specialties: Home-style cooking

*The Wildflower Cafe in Incline Village takes its name from the abundant variety of wildflowers in the surrounding mountains of the Sierra. The traveler who comes across the Wildflower Cafe is just as delighted as the hiker who discovers a lovely flower on the trail, for the home-style cooking fills not only the physical hunger, but a need, when you're on vacation, to eat at a friend's house - that's the atmosphere of The Wildflower. A favorite of the locals, The Wildflower also sees the skiers return each winter for their wonderful muffins and perfectly-cooked eggs, their rich homemade soups and chili made from scratch. Specials change daily, and you may be fortunate to hit the Philly Cheese Steak, not an easy meal to find on Tahoe's North Shore.*

# Salsa

| | |
|---|---|
| 1 | 28-oz. can tomatoes, diced |
| 1 | 4-oz. can diced green chilies |
| 1 | tsp. parsley, chopped |
| 1 | tsp. cilantro, chopped |
| 1/4 | medium onion, diced |
| 1/4 | tsp. red pepper, crushed |
| 1/4 | tsp. salt |
| | dash Tabasco |
| | dash black pepper |
| | dash garlic powder |
| 1 1/2 | tsp. Worcestershire sauce |
| 1 | tsp. oregano leaves |
| | pinch basil |
| | pinch tarragon |

Mix all ingredients, serve with chips or as sauce for tacos.

*Yields 4 cups*

# Carrot Soup

| | |
|---|---|
| 10-12 | carrots, cut in chunks |
| 1 | onion |
| 2 | celery stalks |
| | mace or nutmeg to taste |
| 2 | Tbsp. brown sugar |
| 1/4 | c. butter |
| 1 | c. cream |
| | salt and pepper to taste |

## Carrot Soup (Cont.)

Clean vegetables. In large pot, boil 2 quarts water, add vegetables to boiling water. Add mace or nutmeg and brown sugar. Boil until vegetables are soft. Remove celery and onion. Puree soup. Add butter, cream, salt and pepper. Serve hot.

*Serves 8*

# Pasta Primavera

| | |
|---|---|
| 1 | chicken breast, diced |
| 2 | Tbsp. butter |
| 2 | cloves garlic, minced |
| 1/2 | medium onion, diced |
| 10 | mushrooms, diced |
| 1 | zucchini, diced |
| 2 | c. cream |
| 1/2 | c. Parmesan cheese |
| 2 | lbs. pasta, cooked |
| | chopped parsley |

In large frying pan cook chicken with butter and garlic. Add vegetables and saute. Add more butter if necessary. Add cream and Parmesan and stir constantly. Cook until sauce is reduced to desired consistency. Serve over pasta and garnish with parsley.

*Serves 8*

Calaveras County

# CHARDONNAY

*Grand Reserve*

Stevenot

PRODUCED AND BOTTLED BY STEVENOT WINERY
MURPHYS, CALAVERAS COUNTY, CALIFORNIA B.W. 4839
ALCOHOL 12.5% BY VOLUME

This Chardonnay combines the lushness of Chardonnay fruit with the complexity of barrel fermentation. Intense flavors and elegant balance make this special wine an excellent dinner companion and will reward patient cellaring.

# The Zephyr

## HOT SPRINGS RESORT

**THE ZEPHYR**
Walley's Hot Springs Resort
1-1/2 miles south of Genoa, Nevada on Foothill Road  (P. O. Box 26)
Genoa, NV   89411
(702)782-8155 or (702)883-6556
Hours:  Until 8 p.m. Dinner Wed., Thurs., Sun.
until 9 p.m. Dinner,  Fri. and Sat.
later reservations can be made.
11:30 a.m. - 3:00 p.m. lunch Wed. through Sat.
10:00 a.m. - 3:00 p.m. Sunday brunch
Credit Cards:  Mastercard, American Express, Visa
Prices: Moderate
Reservations:  Suggested
Specialties:  Continental Cuisine

*Walley's Hot Springs Resort is a great spot for an entire day's worth of fun, and you can't beat The Zephyr Restaurant for atmosphere, attentive service and an imaginative menu. Beautifully appointed with leaded glass, brass and a beamed ceiling, The Zephyr specializes in Continental Cuisine. Banquet facilities are available for large parties, and an award-winning wine list will fit your needs. Located about 1 1/2 miles south of Genoa on Foothill Road, Walley's Hot Springs Resort is worth the trip for a great day of spa-ing and delicious dining.*

# Chicken Chardonnay

| | |
|---|---|
| 3 | oz. flour |
| 1/2 | tsp. salt |
| 1/2 | tsp. pepper |
| 1 | 8-oz. chicken breast, skinned and pounded |
| 1 | oz. butter |
| 1/2 | oz. shallots, finely chopped |
| 2 | oz. mushrooms, sliced |
| 1 | oz. Chardonnay |
| 4 | oz. heavy cream |

Mix flour, salt and pepper. Flour chicken breast. Melt butter in hot saute pan over high flame. Add chicken, shallots and mushrooms. Brown chicken on both sides, add wine. Let simmer over medium flame for 1 minute. Add heavy cream and let cook until cream thickens into a sauce.

*Serves 1*

# Veal Sierra

| 3 | oz. flour |
|---|-----------|
| 1/2 | tsp. salt |
| 1/2 | tsp. pepper |
| 6 | oz. veal, pounded |
| 1 | oz. butter |
| 1/4 | oz. shallots, finely chopped |
| 1/4 | oz. garlic, finely chopped |
| 1/2 | tsp. lemon juice |
| 1 | oz. white wine |
| 1 | artichoke heart, halved |
| 3 | oz. Bernaise Sauce (recipe follows) |

Blend flour, salt and pepper together. Flour veal. Melt butter in hot saute pan. Add shallots and garlic and sear veal on both sides. Add lemon juice and white wine. Lower flame to a simmer and add artichoke heart. Let simmer for 1 minute. Place veal on warm plate. Add artichoke heart on top and and cover with Bernaise Sauce.

*Serves 1*

# Bernaise Sauce

| | |
|---|---|
| 1/2 | oz. fresh tarragon, chopped |
| 2 | oz. white wine |
| 3 | egg yolks |
| 1 | tsp. cool water |
| | dash of Tabasco |
| | dash of white pepper |
| 1 | tsp. lemon juice |
| 1/4 | tsp. Worcestershire Sauce |
| 3 | oz. warm butter (120-140° F.) |

Put tarragon and white wine in a small sauce pan and reduce over medium flame until wine is absorbed. Let cool. Over double boiler, whip egg yolks, water, Tabasco, white pepper, lemon juice and Worcestershire Sauce until eggs start to thicken. Then slowly add butter. Remove bottom from the double boiler and fold in the tarragon reduction.

*Serves 2*

# Sonnie's
# Favorite Recipes

# Pea, Pear and Watercress Soup

| | |
|---|---|
| 3 | lbs. peas |
| 1 | lb. pears, cut in 1/2" slices |
| 1 | Tbsp. cooking sherry |
| 1/2 | tsp. nutmeg |
| 2 | bunches watercress |
| 1 | medium onion, diced |
| 4 | Tbsp. butter |
| 7 | c. chicken stock |

In a large saucepan combine peas, pears and cooking sherry, simmer for 1/2 hour. Add nutmeg and watercress, simmer 15 minutes more. Meanwhile, in a saute pan, saute onions in butter until they are soft, not brown. Combine the onions with the vegetables and fruit and puree in batches. Return the pureed ingredients to the saucepan and slowly add the chicken stock. Bring to a boil and simmer 15 minutes.

*Serves 8*

# Chili Rellenos Soup

| | |
|---|---|
| 2 | Tbsp. butter |
| 1 | onion, minced |
| 1 | 28-oz. can tomatoes |
| 1 | 4-oz. can diced green chilies |
| | salt and pepper to taste |
| 1/4 | lb. Cheddar cheese, grated |
| 1/4 | lb. Jack cheese, grated |
| 1/4 | lb. Dofino cheese, grated |

### Chili Rellenos Soup (Cont.)

In a 2 quart saucepan, melt butter. Add onions, simmer until soft. Add tomatoes, green chilies, salt and pepper. Simmer 30 minutes. Stir in cheeses and continue cooking on simmer until the cheeses are melted. Serve immediately.

*Serves 5*

# Tomato Soup

| | |
|---|---|
| 4 | Tbsp. butter |
| 3 | Tbsp. flour |
| 1 1/2c. | milk, scalded |
| 1 | 14 1/2 oz. can Swanson's Chicken Broth, heated |
| 2 | lbs. canned plum tomatoes, pureed |
| 1/2 | c. onions, chopped |
| 1 | Tbsp. honey |
| 1 | Tbsp. parsley, chopped |
| 1/4 | tsp. basil |
| 1/4 | tsp. dill |
| | salt and pepper to taste |

In a 3 quart saucepan, melt butter. Whisk in flour and simmer 3 minutes. Slowly add milk and chicken broth, whisking constantly until it is thick. Add pureed tomatoes, onions, honey, parsley, basil, dill, salt and pepper. Simmer 1/2 hour.

*Serves 6*

# Quick Cream of Broccoli Soup

| | |
|---|---|
| 2 | Tbsp. butter |
| 1 | onion, diced |
| 3 | Tbsp. flour |
| 6 | c. chicken broth |
| 1 | 10 oz. pkg. broccoli, thawed |
| 2 | c. milk |

In a 3 quart saucepan melt butter, add onions and cook until soft. Whisk in flour and stir constantly. Add broth and broccoli and bring to a boil. Cover and simmer 10 minutes. Puree in batches in a blender or food processor. Return to pot, add milk, cook until hot but not boiling. Serve immediately.

*Serves 6*

# Gazpacho

| | |
|---|---|
| 4 | ripe tomatoes, peeled and seeded |
| 1 | green pepper, cut in quarters |
| 2 | garlic cloves |
| 1 | Spanish red onion, cut in quarters |
| 12 | oz. cucumber, cut in large cubes |
| 1/2 | c. olive oil |
| 2 | Tbsp. lemon juice |
| 3 | c. tomato juice |
| 1 | tsp. salt |
| 1/2 | tsp. paprika |
| 1 | c. parsley, chives, chervil and tarragon blended together |

### Gazpacho (Cont.)

In a food processor mince tomatoes, green pepper, garlic, red onion and cucumber. Add olive oil, lemon juice, tomato juice, salt, paprika and herbs. Chill and serve in cups or mugs.

*Serves 6*

# Cheesy Garlic Soup

| | |
|---|---|
| 7 | c. chicken broth |
| 1 | head garlic, chopped |
| 4 | Tbsp. butter |
| 4 | Tbsp. flour |
| 1/4 | c. white wine |
| 2 | c. Gruyere cheese, grated |
| 1 | Tbsp. green onions, minced |
| 1 | Tbsp. cooked bacon, minced |

In a large saucepan bring chicken broth and garlic to a boil. Cover and simmer 15 minutes. Meanwhile, in a stockpot melt butter, stir in flour and gradually add chicken stock, stirring after each addition. Simmer for 15 minutes. Add wine, Gruyere and green onions. Add minced bacon for garnish.

*Serves 6*

# Black Bean Soup

| | |
|---|---|
| 1/2 | lb. black turtle beans |
| 4 | c. water |
| 3/4 | c. onions, chopped |
| 1/2 | c. green pepper, chopped |
| 1/2 | c. carrots, chopped |
| 1/2 | c. celery, chopped |
| 1 | smoked pork hock |
| 4 | c. chicken stock |
| 1 | tsp. salt |
| 1 | tsp. dried thyme |
| 1 | tsp. dry mustard |
| 2 | cloves garlic, minced |
| 1/2 | tsp. pepper |

In a large stockpot soak beans in water 24 hours. To the beans and water, add onions, green pepper, carrots, celery and pork hock. Heat to a boil. Skim, reduce heat to simmer and add chicken stock, salt, thyme, mustard, garlic and pepper. Cover and cook until the beans are tender, about 4 hours.

*Serves 8*

# Cheddar Cheese Soup

| | |
|---|---|
| 1/4 | c. scallions, diced |
| 1/2 | stick butter |
| 3 | Tbsp. flour |
| 3 | c. chicken broth, heated |
| 3/4 | c. carrots, diced |
| | salt and pepper to taste |
| 2 | c. Cheddar cheese, grated |
| 1 | c. milk, scalded |

In a large saucepan saute scallions in butter until they are softened. Stir in flour and whisk for 3 minutes. Add chicken broth and whisk until smooth. Add carrots, salt and pepper and cook the mixture over moderate heat 20 minutes or until the carrots are soft. Stir in Cheddar cheese and milk and cook until the cheese is melted. Simmer the soup for 5 minutes. Serve immediately.

*Serves 6*

# White Clam Chowder

| | |
|---|---|
| 2 | large onions, chopped |
| 3 | Tbsp. butter |
| 2 | large potatoes, diced |
| 2 | 8 oz. bottles clam juice |
| 2 | cans minced clams |
| | salt and pepper to taste |
| | chopped parsley, or |
| | chopped chives |

In a large saucepan saute onions in butter until they are tender but not brown.  Add potatoes and clam juice.  Cook the mixture over gentle heat until the potatoes are tender but still hold their shape.  Add the minced clams and simmer the chowder for a few minutes.  Season with salt and pepper.  Sprinkle with chopped parsley or chives just before serving.

*Serves 4*

# Cream of Celery Soup

| | |
|---|---|
| 10 | c. chicken stock |
| 12 | stalks celery, diced |
| 1/8 | c. white wine |
| 1 | tsp. dried dill |
| 1/2 | tsp. savory |
| 1/2 | tsp. thyme |
| 8 | Tbsp. butter (1 stick) |
| 2 | onions, diced |
| 2 | carrots, diced |

## Cream of Celery Soup (Cont.)

| | |
|---|---|
| 2 | cloves garlic, diced |
| 3/4 | c. unbleached white flour |
| 12 | oz. cream |
| | salt and pepper to taste |

Place chicken stock in a stock pot and bring to a boil. Add celery, wine, dill, savory and thyme. Cool and puree. Return the puree to stock pot and keep warm. Melt butter in a large saucepan. Add onions and carrots and saute for 10 minutes. Add garlic and reduce to simmer, add flour, whisking constantly for 5 minutes. Whisk into stock mixture. Bring to a boil and add cream, heat, but don't boil. Add salt and pepper and serve.

*Serves 10*

# Tomato Bisque

| | |
|---|---|
| 2 | Tbsp. olive oil |
| 4 | oz. butter |
| 1/2 | tsp. dried dill |
| 1/2 | tsp. dried basil |
| 1 | onion, sliced |
| 2 | 28 oz. cans whole tomatoes |
| 3 | Tbsp. tomato paste |
| 5 | c. chicken stock |
| 3 | Tbsp. flour |
| 1 | tsp. honey |

### Tomato Bisque (Cont.)

Melt oil and butter in stock pot. Add next 3 ingredients, cook until onions are soft. Add tomatoes and tomato paste and simmer for 15 minutes. tAdd chicken stock, flour and honey. Simmer for 45 minutes. Puree soup in blender or food processor. Return to stock pot. Cook for 5 more minutes and serve.

*Serves 6*

# Cantonese Pickled Carrots and Turnips

| | |
|---|---|
| 1 | carrot, sliced |
| 1 | turnip, sliced |
| 1 | onion, sliced |
| 1 | Tbsp. salt |
| 1/4 | tsp. pepper |
| 1/2 | c. white vinegar |
| 1/2 | c. water |
| 1/2 | c. sugar |

In a large bowl, combine sliced vegetables. Sprinkle with salt and pepper and let sit at room temperature for 6 hours. Combine vinegar, water and sugar and pour over vegetables. Let sit at room temperature for 12 hours. Place in screw-top jar and refrigerate.

*Serves 8*

# Tomato Salad

| | |
|---|---|
| 6 | large, firm tomatoes, sliced very thin |
| 2 | red onions, sliced thin |
| 4 | tsp. sugar |
| | salt and pepper to taste |

*Marinade:*

| | |
|---|---|
| 1/2 | c. wine vinegar |
| 1/3 | c. olive oil |
| 4 | tsp. dried basil |
| 2 | tsp. dried tarragon |
| 1/4 | tsp. dried oregano |

Combine marinade ingredients in a bowl and stir. In serving bowl, place 1/2 tomatoes and 1/2 onions. Drizzle on 1/2 marinade and repeat with remaining ingredients. Serve chilled.

*Serves 6*

301

# Helen's Seven Layer Salad

| | |
|---|---|
| 1 | head lettuce, shredded |
| 1/4 | c. celery, sliced |
| 1/4 | c. green pepper, diced |
| 1/4 | c. green onions, sliced |
| 1 | 10 oz. pkg. frozen peas, thawed |
| 2 | c. Miracle Whip salad dressing |
| 4 | tsp. sugar |
| 1/4 | lb. grated Cheddar cheese |
| 10 | oz. bacon, fried and crumbled on top |

Layer in order. Refrigerate and serve.

*Serves 5*

# Tabbouleh

| | |
|---|---|
| 1 1/2 | c. Bulghur wheat* |
| 4 | c. boiling water |
| 4 | cloves garlic |
| 1/2 | c. fresh parsley |
| 4 | green onions, cut in 1" pieces |
| 1 | cucumber, peeled and cut in 1" pieces |
| 2 | tomatoes, cut in quarters |
| 1/4 | c. soy sauce |
| 1/4 | c. tamari* |
| 2 | lemons, juiced |
| 1/2 | c. rice vinegar** |

## Tabbouleh (Cont.)

| | |
|---|---|
| 1/4 | c. olive oil |
| 2 | Tbsp. mint |
| | romaine lettuce |

In a large mixing bowl, combine Bulghur wheat and boiling water. Let stand 2 to 3 hours or until Bulghur is soft. Add more water if needed. Drain and set aside. In a food processor, drop in garlic, parsley, green onions, cucumber and tomatoes. Blend. Add remaining ingredients except lettuce and blend well. Add the seasonings to the Bulghur wheat and mix well. Refrigerate for 3 hours and serve with romaine lettuce, which is used as a scoop for the Tabbouleh.

*Available in health food section of grocery

**Available in Oriental markets

*Serves 12*

# Cabbage Salad Angelika

| | |
|---|---|
| 8 | oz. herb vinegar |
| 4 | oz. salad oil |
| 4 1/2 | oz. sugar |
| 1 | Tbsp. salt |
| 1 | Tbsp. mustard seed |
| 3 1/2 | lbs. white cabbage, thinly shredded |
| 2 | medium onions, minced |

### Cabbage Salad Angelika (Cont.)

Bring vinegar, oil, sugar, salt and mustard seed to a boil. Pour over raw shredded cabbage. Add onions. Chill for several hours before serving.

*Serves 10*

# Chili Chicken Salad

| | |
|---|---|
| 1/4 | c. white wine vinegar |
| 1/8 | c. vegetable oil |
| 1/8 | c. sesame oil (available in Oriental Markets) |
| 1 | tsp. lemon juice |
| 2 | c. diced, cooked chicken |
| 1 | head lettuce, chopped |
| 1 | tomato, chopped |
| 1/2 | c. Cheddar cheese, grated |
| 1/2 | c. Monterey Jack cheese, grated |
| 4 | oz. diced green chilies |

Combine vinegar, oils and lemon juice. Set aside. Toss remaining ingredients in a wooden salad bowl. Pour dressing over and toss again.

*Serves 6*

# B. R.'s Chinese Chicken Salad

| | |
|---|---|
| 1 | large head lettuce |
| 1 | c. chicken, cooked and cubed |
| 1 | bunch green onions, sliced thin |
| 2 | oz. sliced almonds |
| 4 | oz. dried Chinese noodles |
| 1/2 | oz. sesame seeds, pan fried |
| 1 | oz. diced mushrooms |
| 1 | c. oil |
| 1 | c. white vinegar |
| 1/4 | c. sugar |
| | salt and pepper to taste |

Mix first seven ingredients together in a large salad bowl. Blend the rest of the ingredients together and pour over salad.

*Serves 8*

# Pesto

| | |
|---|---|
| 1/2 | c. fresh basil |
| 1/2 | c. fresh parsley |
| 2 | cloves garlic |
| 1/4 | c. Parmesan cheese |
| 1/4 | c. olive oil |
| 1/4 | c. pine nuts |

In a food processor combine basil, parsley and garlic. Mix well. Add Parmesan cheese, olive oil and pine nuts. Blend until mixture becomes a thick paste. Chill for 1 hour.

*Yields 2 cups*

# Spinach Dip

| | |
|---|---|
| 2 | c. fresh spinach, chopped |
| 2 | c. fresh parsley, chopped |
| 1 | c. mayonnaise |
| 1 | c. sour cream |
| 1 | c. water chestnuts, chopped |
| 1 | c. onions, chopped |
| 1 | pkg. Knorr Swiss leek soup mix |

Blend all ingredients together and chill for at least 24 hours. Serve with crudites or corn chips.

*Yields 8 cups*

# Shallot and Tarragon Salad Dressing

| | |
|---|---|
| 1 1/2 | c. olive oil |
| 1/2 | c. red wine vinegar |
| 2 | tsp. dried tarragon |
| 3 | shallots, minced |
| 1 | Tbsp. Dijon mustard |
| | salt and pepper to taste |

Combine all ingredients in a screw-top jar and shake. Pour over mixed salad.

*Yields 2 cups*

# Clam Dip

| | |
|---|---|
| 8 | oz. cream cheese, softened |
| 6 1/2 | oz. can minced clams, drained |
| 1/2 | tsp. salt |
| 1/4 | tsp. pepper |
| 1 | Tbsp. Worcestershire Sauce |
| 1/2 | tsp. seasoned salt |

Blend all ingredients together and serve with chips or fresh vegetables.

*Yields 2 cups*

# Salsa

| | |
|---|---|
| 1 | large can plum tomatoes, drained |
| 1 | large can whole tomatoes, drained |
| 1 | onion, diced |
| 2 | green onions, minced |
| 2 | cloves garlic, minced |
| 1 | tsp. coriander |
| 1 | tsp. sugar |
| 1/2 | bottle La Victoria's taco sauce |

Blend all ingredients together in a food processor and refrigerate. Serve with corn chips.

*Yields 5 cups*

# Aioli

3     cloves garlic
1     egg
1     Tbsp. Minute Maid 100% lemon juice
1     tsp. salt
1 1/2  c. olive oil
1     Tbsp. hot water

In a food processor, mince garlic, add egg, lemon juice and salt. With machine running, pour olive oil into the drip tube of the processor (usually the pusher has a small hole in it to allow the olive oil to drip slowly into the processor). When thick, add hot water. Serve with French bread, potatoes, fresh raw vegetables, tomatoes, artichokes or cooked vegetables.

*Yields 1 1/2 cups*

# Kumquat Chutney

3/4    lb. fresh kumquats
2 1/2  c. sugar
2     c. onions, chopped
2     c. cider vinegar
1 1/2  c. golden raisins
4     cloves garlic, minced
1     tsp. whole mustard seed
5     pieces candied ginger

### Kumquat Chutney (Cont.)

In a food processor, chop kumquats. Transfer to a 3 quart sauce pan. Add remaining ingredients and cook uncovered on simmer for 1 1/2 to 2 hours, stirring frequently. Refrigerate and serve as a relish.

*Yield: 6 cups*

# Barbecue Sauce

2    c. catsup
1    c. Worcestershire Sauce
1    c. soy sauce
1    c. packed brown sugar
2    Tbsp. liquid smoke
2    Tbsp. tomato paste
2    cloves garlic, minced
     salt and pepper

Mix all ingredients until well blended. Place in refrigerator for 2 hours before using.

*Yield: 5 cups*

# Eggplant and Cheese

| | |
|---|---|
| 2 | eggplants, peeled and diced |
| 1 | c. water |
| 2 | Tbsp. olive oil |
| 1 | Tbsp. butter |
| 2 | onions, sliced |
| 1/2 | c. water |
| 2 | c. Jack cheese |
| 4 | eggs, beaten |
| | salt and pepper |

In a large frying pan, cook eggplant in 1 c. water until boiling. Cover pan and simmer 15 minutes. Drain eggplant and set aside. In same frying pan, heat oil and butter, add onions and 1/2 c. water. Cook 15 minutes on medium. Add eggplant, cheese, eggs, salt and pepper. Mix well and transfer to a buttered au gratin dish. Bake for 45 to 60 minutes at 375° F.

*Serves 6*

# Baked Garlic Tomatoes

| | |
|---|---|
| 10 | medium tomatoes |
| 2 | Tbsp. olive oil |
| 2 | Tbsp. garlic, minced |
| 2 | Tbsp. parsley, minced |
| 2 | Tbsp. bread crumbs |
| 1/4 | tsp. salt |

## Baked Garlic Tomatoes (Cont.)

Cut tomatoes in half horizontally. Place tomatoes, cut side up, in a baking dish. Drizzle with olive oil and bake at 400° F. for 10 minutes. While they are baking, combine garlic, parsley, bread crumbs and salt. Sprinkle over tomatoes and bake for another 15 minutes.

*Serves 5*

# Baked Grated Potatoes

| | |
|---|---|
| 4 | potatoes, peeled and grated |
| 2 | onions, chopped |
| 1 | c. milk |
| 1/4 | c. Cheddar cheese, grated |
| 1 1/2 | tsp. flour |
| 1 | tsp. salt |
| 1/8 | tsp. pepper |

Place potatoes and onions in a bowl, add milk. Stir in Cheddar cheese, flour, salt and pepper. Transfer the mixture to a buttered baking dish and bake at 350° F. for 2 1/2 hours.

*Serves 4*

# Stuffed Potatoes

6      baking potatoes
1/2    c. green onions, chopped
1/2    lb. bacon, cooked and crumbled
1/2    lb. Cheddar cheese
       Ranch dressing

Bake 6 potatoes. When done, split and scoop out at least 1/2 of each potato. Add green onions, bacon and cheese. Place on baking sheet and bake at 350° F. for 15 minutes. Use Ranch dressing as a dip.

*Serves 6*

# Spinach and Garlic

1/4    lb. butter
1      large onion, chopped
1      head garlic, minced
       salt and pepper
2      lbs. fresh spinach
1/4    lb. Jack cheese, grated
1/2    lb. Cheddar cheese, grated
1/4    c. bread crumbs

In a large frying pan, melt butter, add onions and cook until soft. Add garlic, salt, pepper and spinach and cook for 5 minutes. Add Jack and Cheddar cheese and cook until the cheese melts. Transfer to a buttered casserole dish and sprinkle with bread crumbs. Bake at 350° F. for 35 minutes.

*Serves 6*

# No Crust Quiche

| | |
|---|---|
| 1 | lb. bacon, diced |
| 4 | c. chopped onions |
| 16 | eggs |
| 2 | tsp. salt |
| 1 | tsp. pepper |
| 1/2 | tsp. nutmeg |
| 6 | c. milk |
| 2 | lbs. Gruyere cheese, diced |

Saute bacon until partially cooked. Add onions and cook until tender. Pour off most of the bacon fat. Set aside. Combine eggs, salt, pepper and nutmeg. Beat well. Add milk and blend. Spread onion mixture into 4 pie pans. Sprinkle evenly with cheese. Pour egg mixture over cheese. Bake at 375° F. for 35 to 45 minutes or until knife comes out clean.

*Serves 32*

# Chili Quiche

| | |
|---|---|
| 1/4 | lb. butter, melted |
| 5 | eggs, beaten |
| 1/4 | c. flour |
| 1/2 | tsp. baking powder |
| 1 | 4 oz. can diced green chilies |
| 1 | c. cottage cheese |
| 8 | oz. Jack cheese, grated |

Combine all ingredients. Pour into a 12" x 9" baking dish. Bake at 350° F. for 35 minutes. Cool and cut into squares.

# Green Chili Tesquaquas

3      flour tortillas
2      oz. Jack cheese, grated
1      oz. Gruyere cheese, grated
1      green onion, diced
2      oz. diced green chilies
5      tsp. sour cream
4      Tbsp. green taco sauce

In a casserole layer 1 tortilla, 1/3 cheese, green onion, chilies and sour cream. Repeat 2 more times. Pour green taco sauce on top. Place in microwave for 4 minutes on high or until cheese is melted and bubbly.

*Serves 2*

# Lasagna

1       lb. ground beef
1       small onion, diced
1       28-oz. can tomatoes
1       12-oz. can tomato paste
1       Tbsp. sugar
1 1/2  tsp. salt
1/2     tsp. dried oregano
1/2     tsp. dried thyme
1/8     tsp. pepper

## Lasagna (Cont.)

| | |
|---|---|
| 1 | clove garlic, minced |
| 1 | bay leaf |
| 1 | 16 oz. package lasagna noodles, cooked and drained |
| 2 | eggs, beaten |
| 1 | 15 oz. package ricotta cheese |
| 1 | lb. mozzarella cheese, diced |

In a large frying pan, cook ground beef and onions until beef is brown. Add tomatoes, tomato paste, sugar, salt, oregano, thyme, pepper, garlic and bay leaf. Heat until boiling. Reduce to simmer and cook for 30 minutes, stirring occasionally. Discard bay leaf. In a greased 13" x 9" baking dish, arrange half the lasagna noodles, overlapping to fit dish. Combine eggs and ricotta cheese. Spoon 1/2 mixture over noodles and sprinkle with 1/2 of the mozzarella cheese. Top with 1/2 sauce mixture. Repeat. Bake at 375° F. for 45 minutes

*Serves 8*

# Macaroni and Cheese

| | |
|---|---|
| 1/2 | lb. macaroni, cooked |
| 1/2 | c. mozzarella cheese, grated |
| 1/2 | c. Gruyere cheese, grated |
| 1/4 | c. Parmesan cheese, grated |
| 1/4 | c. Fontina cheese, grated |
| 1/4 | c. parsley, minced |
| 3 | Tbsp. butter, melted |

Place cooked macaroni in a buttered 1 1/2 quart baking dish. Add cheeses, parsley and butter. Bake at 375° F. for 20 minutes.

*Serves 4 to 6*

# Linguine with Clam Sauce

| | |
|---|---|
| 1/4 | c. butter |
| 1 | onion, diced |
| 3 | cloves garlic, minced |
| 1 | tsp. flour |
| 2 | 6 1/2 oz. cans minced clams |
| 2 | Tbsp. parsley, minced |
| | salt and pepper |
| 8 | oz. linguine, cooked |

In a medium saucepan, melt butter over medium heat. Add onions and garlic and cook until soft. Whisk in flour. Add clams and simmer, covered for 10 minutes. Add parsley, salt and pepper. Serve over linguine.

*Serves 2*

# Linguine and Tomatoes

| | |
|---|---|
| 1 | small can plum tomatoes |
| 1/2 | c. olive oil |
| 1 | clove garlic, minced |
| 1 | c. basil leaves, chopped |
| 1 | lb. linguine, cooked |

Combine tomatoes, olive oil, garlic and basil.  Pour over cooled linguine.

*Serves 2*

# Rice Casserole

| | |
|---|---|
| 3/4 | c. rice, cooked |
| 2 | c. sour cream |
| 1 | 7-oz. can minced green chili peppers |
| 3/4 | lb. Jack cheese |

Mix cooked rice together with sour cream.  Place 1/2 of rice mixture into a buttered casserole.  Add 1/2 chili peppers, 1/2 cheese.  Repeat.  Bake uncovered at 350° F. for 45 minutes.

*Serves 4 to 6*

# Three Bean Casserole

| | |
|---|---|
| 1 | large onion, chopped and browned in bacon fat |
| 1 | large can B & M Baked Beans |
| 1 | medium can kidney beans |
| 1 | medium can lima beans |
| 1 | clove garlic, minced |
| 1/2 | c. catsup |
| 3 | Tbsp. brown sugar |
| 1 | tsp. dry mustard |
| 1 | tsp. salt |
| 1 | tsp. Worcestershire Sauce |

Mix all ingredients together and bake in preheated 350° F. oven for 1 hour.

*Serves 10*

# Baked Creole Whitefish

| | |
|---|---|
| 1 | c. tomato sauce |
| 3 | Tbsp. parsley, chopped |
| 1/2 | tsp. Creole seasoning (recipe follows) |
| 1 | clove garlic, minced |
| 2 | tsp. fine herbs |
| 2 | lbs. whitefish fillets (catfish, orange roughy, sole etc.) |
| 4 | Tbsp. Parmesan cheese, grated |

Combine first 5 ingredients together. Place fish in casserole dish. Pour sauce over top of fish and sprinkle with Parmesan cheese. Let it marinate for 1/2 hour. Bake at 350° F. for 1/2 hour.

*Serves 6*

# Creole Seasoning

| | |
|---|---|
| 1 | Tbsp. salt |
| 1 | Tbsp. red pepper |
| 1 | Tbsp. black pepper |
| 1 | Tbsp. garlic powder |
| 1 | Tbsp. chili powder |

Combine all ingredients together.

# Garlic Trout

| | |
|---|---|
| 2 | 10 oz. trout |
| | salt and pepper |
| 1/4 | c. butter, softened |
| 1 | clove garlic, minced |
| 1 | tsp. shallots, minced |
| 1 | Tbsp. fresh parsley, minced |
| 1/4 | c. dry vermouth |

Sprinkle trout with salt and pepper. In a bowl, combine butter, garlic, shallots and parsley. Place mixture in the trouts cavity. Place fish in baking dish and pour in wine. Bake, covered with a buttered sheet of waxed paper and a sheet of tin foil, at 400° F. for 20 minutes.

*Serves 4*

# Scallops Seviche

| | |
|---|---|
| 1 1/2 | lbs. scallops |
| 1/2 | c. lime juice |
| 1/2 | c. fresh parsley, minced |
| 1/4 | c. olive oil |
| 8 | green onions, sliced |
| 1 | small red onion, chopped |
| 1 | clove garlic, minced |
| 2 | medium tomatoes, diced |
| 2 | oz. diced green chili peppers |

In a ceramic bowl combine scallops and lime juice. Cover and refrigerate overnight. Stir occasionally. Drain and add remaining ingredients. Refrigerate 12 hours before serving.

*Serves 6 to 8*

# Caesar Burgers

| | |
|---|---|
| 1 | lb. ground beef |
| 1/4 | c. Parmesan cheese, grated |
| 1 | Tbsp. anchovy fillets, minced |
| 1 | egg |
| 2 | tsp. lemon juice |
| 1 | tsp. Worcestershire Sauce |
| 1/4 | c. olive oil |
| 2 | cloves garlic, crushed |
| 4 | hamburger buns |

### Caesar Burgers (Cont.)

Mix beef, cheese, anchovy, egg, lemon juice and Worcestershire sauce in a medium bowl. Shape into 4 hamburger patties. Heat oil and garlic in large skillet until garlic is golden. Remove garlic. Pan fry patties in same skillet over medium-high heat 4 minutes on each side. Place over hamburger buns.

*Serves 4*

# Stuffed Cabbage

| | |
|---|---|
| 1 | head cabbage |
| 1 | lb. ground beef |
| 1 | egg |
| 1 | onion, diced |
| 1/4 | c. bread crumbs |
| | salt and pepper to taste |
| 1 | onion, diced |
| 1/4 | c. oil |
| 1 | small can tomato paste |
| 1 | medium can whole tomatoes |
| 1 | Tbsp. lemon juice |
| 1 | Tbsp. sugar |
| 4 | ginger snaps, crumbled |

Loosen leaves of cabbage and pour boiling water over it, soaking until the leaves are soft. Meanwhile in a large bowl, mix ground beef, egg, 1 onion, bread crumbs, salt and pepper. Roll 2 Tbsp. meat mixture in each cabbage leaf and roll, tucking the top and bottom in. Set aside. In a large saucepan, cook remaining onion in oil until soft.

### Stuffed Cabbage (Cont.)

Add tomato paste and whole tomatoes and bring to a boil. Reduce to simmer and add lemon juice, sugar and ginger snaps. Mix well. Place stuffed cabbage leaves on top of sauce and simmer, covered for 2 hours.

*Serves 4*

# Chili

| | |
|---|---|
| 1 | Tbsp. oil |
| 1 | large onion, diced |
| 1 | green pepper, diced |
| 1 | stalk celery, diced |
| 2 | cloves garlic, diced |
| 1 | large can kidney beans |
| 4 | lbs. ground beef |
| 1 | large can tomato sauce |
| 1 | large can stewed tomatoes |
| 3 | oz. tomato paste |
| 2 | oz. chili salsa |
| 3 | oz. chili powder |
| 4 | oz. diced green chilies |
| | salt and pepper to taste |

In a large stock pot, heat oil, add onions, green pepper, celery and garlic. Cook until soft. Add beans and ground meat. Add remaining ingredients and cook on medium heat until bubbling. Reduce to simmer and continue cooking, covered, for 3 hours. Stir occasionally.

*Serves 8*

# Chinese Tomato Beef

| | |
|---|---|
| 1/4 | c. soy sauce |
| 2 | Tbsp. fresh ginger, grated |
| 2 | cloves garlic, minced |
| 1 | tsp. cornstarch |
| 1 | tsp. sugar |
| 1 | lb. flank steak, thinly sliced |
| 3 | Tbsp. peanut oil |
| 1 | lb. medium tomatoes, quartered |
| 4 | stalks celery, cut into 1" pieces |
| 6 | green onions, cut into 1/2" pieces |
| 1 | green pepper, cut into 1" pieces |
| 1 | onion, cut into small chunks |
| 2 | tsp. cornstarch |
| 3/4 | c. soy sauce |

Combine first 5 ingredients in a large bowl. Add meat and marinate for 30 minutes. Heat 2 Tbsp. oil in wok over high heat. Add meat and stir-fry for about 2 minutes. Remove meat. Add remaining oil to wok and add vegetables. Stir-fry 5 minutes. Reduce heat, add cornstarch dissolved in soy sauce. Cook until sauce is thickened. Add meat and simmer for another 2 minutes.

*Serves 4*

# German-Style Short Ribs

| | |
|---|---|
| 1 | c. catsup |
| 1 | c. water |
| 2 | Tbsp. brown sugar |
| 2 | Tbsp. rice vinegar |
| 1 | Tbsp. Worcestershire Sauce |
| 1 | Tbsp. dry mustard |
| 1 | Tbsp. white horseradish |
| 1/2 | tsp. allspice |
| 2 | onions, chopped |
| 4 | lbs. short ribs |
| 1/2 | c. ginger snaps, crumbled |

Blend together first 9 ingredients in a plastic bag. Add short ribs and marinate in refrigerator for at least 36 hours, turning the bag a few times. Place ribs and marinade in an ovenproof casserole and bake at 350° F. for 3 hours or until the ribs are tender. Remove ribs from casserole. Skim off fat from juices. Stir in crushed ginger snaps and return ribs to thickened gravy. Turn ribs and serve immediately.

*Serves 4*

# Sauerbraten

| | |
|---|---|
| 3 | lbs. steak |
| 1 | tsp. salt |
| 1/8 | tsp. pepper |
| 1 | c. carrots, sliced |
| 2 | c. onions, sliced |
| 1/2 | c. celery, chopped |
| 3 | cloves garlic |
| 3 | peppercorns |
| 1 | c. red wine vinegar |
| 1 | bay leaf |
| 4 | c. water |
| 2 | Tbsp. oil |
| 6 | Tbsp. butter |
| 3 | Tbsp. flour |
| 1 | Tbsp. brown sugar |
| 6 | ginger snaps, crushed |

Place steak in a ceramic baking dish. Add next 10 ingredients. Cover and refrigerate for 3 days, turning meat each day. Remove meat from marinade. Saute meat in oil, add marinade and bring to a boil. Simmer for 3 hours. In a sauce pan, melt butter and stir in flour with a whisk. Add sugar and brown. Add this mixture to the simmering meat. Cover and cook for 1 more hour. Stir in crushed ginger snaps and cook until thickened.

*Serves 6*

# Hoisin Chicken

| | |
|---|---|
| 2 | cloves garlic |
| 1 | Tbsp. fresh ginger |
| 6 | green onions |
| 1 | Tbsp. lemon peel |
| 3 | Tbsp. catsup |
| 3 | Tbsp. honey |
| 3 | Tbsp. soy sauce |
| 2 | Tbsp. rice vinegar* |
| 3 | Tbsp. hoisin* |
| 1/2 | tsp. salt |
| 1/2 | tsp. pepper |
| 5 | lbs. chicken thighs |

Place everything but chicken in a food processor and blend together.  Place chicken in a plastic bag.  Add all blended ingredients to plastic bag and marinate overnight in refrigerator.  Preheat oven to 425° F.  Remove chicken from plastic bag and bake in a single layer covered with foil for 50 minutes, turning once with a fork.  Uncover and continue baking for 10 more minutes.

*Available in Oriental markets

*Serves 8*

# Honey Chicken

| | |
|---|---|
| 3 | lbs. chicken pieces |
| 1 | small onion, chopped |
| 3 | Tbsp. honey |
| 2 | Tbsp. soy sauce |
| 1 | Tbsp. ginger, minced |
| 1 | clove garlic, minced |
| 4 | green onions, chopped |

Place chicken pieces in baking dish. Add next 5 ingredients and marinate for 2 hours. Bake at 425° F. for 45 minutes or until chicken is done. Add green onions and serve.

*Serves 4 to 6*

# Chili Chicken Casserole

| | |
|---|---|
| 1/2 | c. onions, chopped |
| 2 | Tbsp. butter |
| 3 | cans cream of mushroom, chicken or celery soup |
| 4 | oz. pimentos, chopped |
| 4 | oz. diced green chilies |
| 16 | oz noodles, cooked |
| 4 | c. chicken, cooked and diced |
| 3 | c. sharp Cheddar cheese, grated |

Heat oven to 350° F. In a saucepan saute onions in butter until soft. Stir in soup, pimentos and chilies. In a buttered 4 quart baking dish, layer 1/2 noodles, chicken, soup mixture and cheese. Repeat. Bake for 45 minutes.

*Serves 12*

# Key Lime Pie

| | |
|---|---|
| 6 | egg yolks |
| 1 | c. lime juice |
| 2 | 14-oz. cans sweetened condensed milk |
| 1 | Tbsp. grated lime rind |
| 1 | 9" graham cracker pie crust |
| | whipped cream |

Beat egg yolks and add lime juice, condensed milk and grated lime rind. Pour into pie shell and freeze. When ready to serve, spread on whipped cream.

*Serves 6*

# Hurry-Up Coffee Cake

| | |
|---|---|
| 1 | egg |
| 1/2 | c. milk |
| 2 | Tbsp. vegetable oil |
| 1 | c. flour |
| 1/2 | c. sugar |
| 2 | tsp. baking soda |
| 1/2 | tsp. salt |

*Topping:*

| | |
|---|---|
| 1/2 | c. brown sugar |
| 2 | tsp. cinnamon |
| 1/2 | c. chopped walnuts (optional) |

### Hurry-Up Coffee Cake (Cont.)

Beat egg and milk together. Add oil. Blend dry ingredients together and stir into mixture. Blend thoroughly. Pour into a greased pan. Sprinkle with topping and bake at 375° F. for 20 to 25 minutes. Serve warm.

*Serves 6*

# Roma's Orange Jello Salad

| | |
|---|---|
| 32 | oz. small curd cottage cheese. |
| 1 | 6-oz. package orange Jello |
| 1 | 20-oz. can crushed pineapple, drained |
| 9 | oz. Cool Whip |
| 1/2 | c. chopped walnuts or pecans |

Place cottage cheese in bowl. Add Jello and mix well. Add pineapple. Fold in Cool Whip. Place nuts on top. Chill and serve.

*Serves 6*

# Sour Cream Coffee Cake

| | |
|---|---|
| 1/4 | lb. butter |
| 1 | c. sugar |
| 2 | eggs |
| 1 | tsp. baking soda |
| 1/2 | c. sour cream |
| 2 | c. flour |
| 1 1/2 | tsp. baking powder |

*Top and Center Crumbs:*

| | |
|---|---|
| 1/2 | c. brown sugar |
| 1 | tsp. cinnamon |
| 12 | walnuts, chopped |
| 1 | tsp. butter |

Cream together butter, sugar and eggs. Combine baking soda and sour cream and add to butter-sugar mixture. Add flour and baking powder. Pour into buttered baking dish. Blend crumb mixture together and swirl 1/2 into the cake. Top cake off with other 1/2 of crumb mixture. Bake at 350° F. for 45 minutes.

*Serves 6*

# Lemon Curd Cheesecake

| | |
|---|---|
| 2 | 8 oz. packages cream cheese |
| 3/4 | c. sugar |
| 2 | Tbsp. flour |
| 1/2 | tsp. salt |
| 3 | eggs, beaten lightly |
| 1 | c. sour cream |
| 1/4 | c. lemon juice |
| 1 | tsp. vanilla |
| 1 | 9" graham cracker crust |
| | lemon curd topping (recipe follows) |

Place cream cheese in food processor. Add sugar, flour and salt. Blend in eggs, sour cream, lemon juice and vanilla. Pour into pie crust and bake at 325° F. until knife inserted in middle of cake comes out clean (about 1 1/4 hours). Cool and ice with lemon curd.

*Serves 6*

# Lemon Curd

| | |
|---|---|
| 2 | egg yolks |
| 2 | Tbsp. butter |
| 1/4 | c. sugar |
| 2 | Tbsp. lemon juice |
| 1/2 | tsp. grated lemon rind |

In a saucepan, combine egg yolks, butter, sugar and lemon juice. Cook over medium heat, stirring until the curd coats the spoon. Add lemon rind and cool for 1 hour in refrigerator.

# Apple and Cheese Pie

| | |
|---|---|
| 3/4 | c. whole wheat flour |
| 3/4 | c. white unbleached flour |
| 3/4 | c. oatmeal |
| 1/3 | c. dark brown sugar |
| 1/2 | c. butter, softened |
| 1 | egg yolk |
| 3 | Granny Smith apples, sliced |
| 1/2 | c. almonds, slivered |
| 1/2 | c. dark brown sugar |
| 1 | tsp. cinnamon |
| 1/4 | tsp. nutmeg |
| 1/2 | c. raisins |
| 2 | c. Cheddar cheese, grated |

Combine flours, oatmeal, 1/3 c. brown sugar and butter. Mix well. In a large mixing bowl, beat egg yolk, add flour mixture and blend well. Using all the dough but 1/2 c., press into a 10" glass pie plate. Bake at 300° F. for 20 minutes. Arrange the apples evenly over the baked crust, cover with foil and bake at 300° F. for 30 minutes. Combine almonds, 1/2 c. sugar, reserved dough, cinnamon and nutmeg for the topping. Sprinkle raisins, cheese and topping mix over the apples. Bake at 350° F. uncovered, for 15 minutes or until the apples are soft.

*Serves 10*

# Scones

| | |
|---|---|
| 2 3/4 | c. unbleached flour |
| 1 | Tbsp. baking powder |
| 1/2 | tsp. baking soda |
| 1/2 | tsp. salt |
| 1/2 | tsp. cinnamon |
| 1/3 | c. sugar |
| 6 | Tbsp. unsalted butter, cut into chunks |
| 1/8 | c. corn oil |
| 1 | c. raisins |
| 2 | eggs |
| 2/3 | c. buttermilk |

In a food processor, blend first 6 ingredients. Add the butter and blend well. Add oil. Transfer to a bowl and add raisins. Mix together the eggs and buttermilk and add to dough. Mix thoroughly. Drop the dough by 1/4 c. measure on a buttered cookie sheet. Bake at 425° F. for 20 minutes or until golden.

*Serves 10*

# Brazilian Lace Cookies

| | |
|---|---|
| 1 1/2 | c. brown sugar |
| 1 | Tbsp. water |
| 1/4 | c. butter |
| 1 | tsp. cinnamon |
| 1 | c. Brazil nuts, chopped |
| 1 | c. flour |

Mix sugar and water together to make a paste. Add butter, cinnamon, nuts and flour. Shape into small rounds, about 1" in diameter, on a greased baking sheet. Place at least 2" apart. Bake at 325° F. for 15 minutes. Remove from heat and let stand for 1 minute. Lift from baking sheet. These can be iced or covered with melted semi-sweet chocolate.

# Deep Dish Apple Crisp

| | |
|---|---|
| 5 | Granny Smith apples, sliced |
| 1 | c. flour |
| 1 | c. sugar |
| 1/4 | lb. butter, melted |
| 1 | tsp. baking powder |
| 1 | egg |
| 1 | tsp. cinnamon |
| 1 | Tbsp. lemon juice |
| 4 | Tbsp. butter, melted |

Place 1/2 apples in a deep baking dish. Combine next 7 ingredients and add 1/2 to apples. Repeat. Pour butter on top and bake at 350° F. for 1 hour.

*Serves 8*

# Banana Cake

| | |
|---|---|
| 3/4 | c. flour |
| 1 | Tbsp. cornstarch |
| 1/2 | tsp. baking powder |
| 1/2 | tsp. baking soda |
| 1/2 | tsp. salt |
| 1/2 | c. butter |
| 1 1/2 | c. sugar |
| 2 | eggs |
| 6 | Tbsp. milk |
| 3 | bananas, mashed |
| 1 | tsp. vanilla |

Sift flour with cornstarch, baking powder, baking soda and salt. Cream butter and sugar together. Add eggs, flour mixture and milk. Add bananas and vanilla. Pour into a 9 x 13 1/2 baking dish. Bake at 350° F. for 30 minutes.

*Serves 8*

# Pecan-Praline Cookies

| | |
|---|---|
| 3 | Tbsp. butter |
| 1 | c. brown sugar |
| 1 | egg, beaten |
| 1 | c. pecan halves |
| 1/4 | c. flour |
| 1 | tsp. vanilla |

In a saucepan, melt butter and stir in brown sugar. Remove the pan from the heat and mix in egg, pecans, flour and vanilla. On a greased cookie sheet, drop dough by tsp. into mounds about 5" apart. Bake at 350° F. for 8 to 10 minutes. Let the cookies stand for 1 minute before lifting off the cookie sheet with a spatula.

*Yields about 30 cookies*

# Lace Cookies

| | |
|---|---|
| 3/4 | c. brown sugar |
| 1/2 | c. butter, softened |
| 2 | Tbsp. flour |
| 2 | Tbsp. milk |
| 1 | tsp. vanilla |
| 1 1/4 | rolled oats |

Cream together the brown sugar and butter. Beat in flour, milk and vanilla. Stir in rolled oats and drop the dough by tsp. on an ungreased cookie sheet, about 2" apart. Bake at 350° F. for 10 minutes. Let the cookies stand for 1 minute and then turn them upside down and roll them into a cylinder shape.

*Yields about 30 cookies*

# Bride's Punch

| | |
|---|---|
| 2 | 6 oz. cans frozen orange juice |
| 1 | 6 oz. can frozen lemonade concentrate |
| 1 | 12 oz. can apricot nectar |
| 2 | c. pineapple juice |
| 7 | c. water |
| 2 1/2 | c. chilled ginger ale |
| 1 | 10 1/2 oz. package sliced frozen strawberries |

Mix orange juice, lemonade, apricot nectar, pineapple juice and water in a punch bowl. Chill. Add ginger ale and mix well. Float strawberries on top.

*Yields about 14 cups*

# GLOSSARY

**AL DENTE:** *Pasta or vegetables cooked only until firm and crunchy, not soft or overdone.*

**BLACK BEAN SAUCE:** *Available in Oriental Markets.*

**BLANCH:** *To briefly heat foods in a large quantity of boiling water and sometimes placed in ice water afterwards to stop the cooking process.*

**BOUQUET GARNI:** *Parsley, thyme and bay leaf tied together to flavor a dish as it cooks and removed before serving.*

**BRAISE:** *To sear meat over high flame in oil and then cook slowly in an oven in a covered dish with a small quantity of liquid.*

**BROWN SAUCE:** *Made from brown roux, brown stock, browned mirepoix, tomatoe puree, and herbs cooked togehter slowly, skimmed and strained.*

**CLARIFIED BUTTER:** *Heat whole butter very slowly. Remove white deposit that forms on top. Strain the butter through a sieve into a small bowl, leaving the milky solids in the bottom of the pan. Store uncovered in refrigerator, as it will keep indefinitely. Butter so treated has a higher burning point.*

**DEGLAZE:** *Pour wine into pan in which food has been prepared in butter (food has been removed and just the pan juices remain).*

**DEMI-GLACE:** *Bring 2 c. veal stock to a boil and simmer until reduced by half.*

**EGG WASH:** *1 egg, beaten with 1 Tbsp. water*

**FUSILLI:** *Thin, spiral-shaped pasta.*

**HOLLANDAISE SAUCE:** *Divide 1/2 c. butter into 3 pieces. Put 1 piece in top of double boiler with 2 egg yolks and 1 Tbsp. lemon juice. Stir constantly with a whisk until butter is melted. Add second piece of butter and then the third piece. Add 1/3 c. boiling water and 1/4 tsp. salt.*

**LIME, ORANGE OR LEMON ZEST:** *The grated outer covering of lemon or lime, just the skin part, as the white part becomes bitter.*

**NORI:** *Thin black sheets of seaweed, used to wrap sushi (available in Oriental markets).*

**REDUCE OR REDUCTION:** *To boil down a liquid and to thicken its consistency and concentrate its flavors.*

**ROUX:** *Mixture of butter and flour. Melt butter in saucepan. Add flour slowly and whisk until thick. This is used to thicken sauces and soups.*

**SEAR:** *To brown the surface of meat quickly with high heat.*

**SPATZLE:** *Noodle or dumpling pressed through a colander.*

**VELOUTE:** *A white sauce based on a white roux with white stock, either fish, chicken, or vegetable.*

**WATER BATH:** *Place the recepticle in which you are cooking the ingredients into a large recepticle, to which an amount of water has been added.*

# Wine Glossary

**ACID** - A naturally occurring and essential component of wine that provides freshness, balance and potential for longevity. A good balance between acid and sugar is sought in the grapes at harvest and in the finished wine.

**AGING** - The process of bringing wine to a point where it is judged ready for market. If storage conditions are right and the wine has the components for longevity, aging can go on for years in the bottle. Red varietal wines usually age well, and some white varietals also can have long lives.

**APPELLATION OF ORIGIN** - The geographical origin of wine, always stated clearly and prominently on the wine label. These geographical regions, or appellations, are designated by the Federal Government based upon several criteria, among them that the area produces grapes and wines that are unique to it in some demonstrable way. The appellation may cover an area as large as the United States and as small or smaller than the Napa Valley.

**AROMA** - The olfactory sensation (smell) of a wine that is directly related to the grape from which it is made (see BOUQUET and NOSE).

**BARREL FERMENTATION** - Meaning that a wine was fermented totally or partially in a small oak barrel.

**BERRY** - The individual grape within a cluster, or bunch, of grapes. A term used interchangeably with grape in the wine and winegrape industry.

**BLEND** - As a noun, blend may refer to any mixture of wines from different varietals, different vintages or different appellations of origin. Within a winery, blend may also refer to a "master blend," wherein specific proportions of different lots of the same wine are used to achieve a particular style or personality of wine.

**BLOOM** - The stage in each growing season, usually late spring or early summer, when grapevines blossom with small flowers and self-pollination occurs.

**BOTRYTIS CINEREA** - A mold that affects grapes when weather conditions are within certain ranges of warmth and humidity. When it occurs late in the growing season under these specific conditions, the mold causes the grape skins to shrivel and brown and the natural grape sugars to concentrate. Under these beneficial conditions, botrytis is called the 'noble rot'. It results in wonderfully luscious and sweet dessert wines that cannot be achieved under any other conditions, either artificial or natural.

# Wine Glossary (con't)

**BOUQUET** - The olfactory sensation of a wine that is a direct result of its cooperage and aging.

**BRIX** - A term used to express a standard measurement of soluble solids (sugar) content in grapes. Expressed as degrees of Brix, it is an indication of ripeness in the grapes and the potential alcohol content of the finished wine.

**BUD** - As a noun, a small node or lump on the mature cane of a grapevine from which shoots grow in the spring. As a verb, refers to the act of budding or grafting wood from one vine onto another.

**BUD BREAK** - An event that signals the beginning of the annual growing season of a grapevine. Usually occurring in late winter or early spring, new buds break through the woody surface of the vine, indicating both the time when the vines will flower and the time when the grapes will reach maturity for harvest.

**CANE** - A mature shoot of one-year-old wood on a grapevine.

**CAP** - A crusty layer of grape skins, pulp and seeds that forms on top of a red varietal wine during fermentation.

**CELLAR** - As a noun, that area within a winery where wines are made and aged. As a verb, refers to cellaring or aging bottled wine.

**CELLARMASTER** - The person who is chief of production in a winery, in charge of operations and looking to the winemaster for direction.

**CHARACTER** - A term for distinguishing features that are collectively an integrated expression of what makes one wine different from another.

**COMPLEXITY** - A term that connotes a number of discernible characteristics in a wine. The overall sensation of a wine, derived from all of its features, its components, its characteristics. Fruit, winemaking style and cooperage are examples of factors that contribute to a wine's complexity.

**COOPERAGE** - Containers of any size or material that hold wine before it is bottled.

**CRUSH** - The activity that occurs immediately after grapes are harvested— they are taken to the winery to be crushed. The terms 'harvest' and 'crush' are frequently used interchangeably to describe the culmination of a growing season, when the grapes are harvested, transported to the winery and made into wine.

# Wine Glossary (con't)

**CUVEE** - A French term applicable primarily to Champagne and sparkling wines. It refers to the specific blend of still wines used in the second fermentation process.

**DRY WINE** - A wine without perceptible sweetness, generally below .5% residual sugar.

**ENOLOGY** - The science of winemaking. Also oenology.

**FERMENTATION** - The process by which yeast converts grape juice to alcohol.

**FILTRATION** - The process of passing wine through a porous material at various stages of development to remove suspended natural solid materials.

**FINING** - A process in which clays or protein, such as raw egg whites, are passed through the wine as clarifying agents. The fining material settles to the bottom, and is removed with the sediments.

**FREE RUN** - The fresh grape juice which is collected and available for fermentation prior to pressing the grapes for further juice extraction.

**FROST PROTECTION** - Various methods for preventing frost from damaging grapevines, by using vineyard heaters, overhead sprinklers or wind machines, individually or in combination.

**GENERIC** - Describes wines not bearing names of the grapes from which they were made. In the U.S., examples of such wines are Chablis, Burgundy or Rosé.

**GONDOLA** - A large, wheeled, open trailer in which grapes are transported from vineyards to wineries for crushing.

**LATE HARVEST** - A term used for grapes that are allowed to stay on vines well past the primary harvest season, with or without Botrytis Cinerea mold. Grape sugars concentrate in the berries through dehydration, resulting in a luscious sweet wine. Late harvest wines vary in sweetness depending upon the sugar content of the grapes at time of harvest. Labeling laws are exacting regarding the use of the terms Late Harvest, Select Late Harvest and Special Select Late Harvest, each of which denotes a minimum harvest sugar level.

**LIMOUSIN** - The name of a government-owned forest in France that is a source of oak used to make cooperage of various sizes for aging wine.

# Wine Glossary (con't)

**METHODE CHAMPENOISE** - The classic method of producing high-quality champagne and sparkling wines in which a second fermentation takes place in the same bottle in which the wine is sold.

**MICROCLIMATE** - An area, generally small, defined by topography, climate, soil type and other environmental elements. A microclimate possesses singular features unto itself which will affect the qualities and character of a wine produced from grapes grown within its borders.

**MUST** - The combination of juice, pulp, seeds and skins of grapes as they leave the crusher and go into the fermentation tank.

**NEVERS** - Another government-owned forest in France that provides oak for wine aging cooperage.

**NOSE** - The overall olfactory sensation of a particular wine, good or bad, encompassing both its aroma (from the grape) and its bouquet (from cooperage and aging).

**pH** - A measurable factor in wine and in grapes that indicates the activity of acid. pH is a factor that controls elements in wine that may lead to longevity and is ultimately the most important factor in choosing the time to harvest grapes.

**PHYLLOXERA VASTATRIX** - A root louse that attacks the roots of grapevines and eventually kills them. In the Napa Valley, and in most of the European wine regions, most vines grow on phylloxera-resistant rootstock.

**POMACE** - The dry residue of skins, seeds and pulp from pressed wine.

**PRESS** - Equipment used to recover either the fresh grape juice after crushing, or wine out of the fermented must, or both.

**PRUNING** - Trimming the dormant grapevines during winter; also called 'removing the brush'. Pruning is the primary method used for managing the crop level, by leaving a pre-determined number of buds on each cane.

**PUMPING OVER** - The act of pumping red wine from the bottom of a fermentation tank into the top of the tank, over the cap, to develop even color extraction and aerate the wine as it ferments, thus aiding fermentation.

**RACKING** - The process of moving wine from one cooperage to another.

# Wine Glossary (con't)

**REFRACTOMETER** - A device that measures the soluble solids (sugar) content of grapes and other fruit, and reads it out in degrees of Brix.

**RESIDUAL SUGAR** - The unfermented grape sugars remaining in a finished wine, indicating its degree of sweetness. Residual sugar is frequently indicated on the wine label by weight or degrees Brix.

**ROOTSTOCK** - The roots and woody stem of non-fruiting grape varieties onto which specific winegrape varieties are grafted. Such rootstock is generally chosen for its resistance to soil pests such as phylloxera or nematodes, but is also selected for its particular growth characteristics, its adaption to particular soils and its affinity for the type of grape to be grown.

**SKIN CONTACT** - Refers to the crushed skins of grapes remaining with the fresh grape juice before pressing. The amount of time allowed for skin contact is a decision that affects some aspects of finished wine, such as color or tannins.

**SPARKLING WINES** - Wines that undergo a second fermentation, usually in the bottle, resulting in effervescence.

**SWEET WINES** - Wines that contain perceptible percentages of residual sugar. The threshold for perceiving sweetness is about .5 to .7% residual sugar. Wine with 1% or more residual sugar will taste sweet. Some of the classic finished dessert wines may have as much as 32% residual sugar.

**TANNIN** - A group of organic substances in grape skins, seeds and stems. Tannin is responsible for the astringent, puckery quality in some young wines. Tannin is present in virtually all wines but is generally more pronounced in red wines.

**TRONCAIS** - Another government-owned forest in France which produces oak for wine cooperage.

**VARIETAL** - A wine produced totally or primarily from one specific grape variety and which bears the name of that variety; Cabernet Sauvignon, Chardonnay, Sauvignon Blanc, Zinfandel, etc. In order to bear that name on its label, the wine must contain a minimum of 75% of the varietal named.

**VARIETY** - The botanical name for a specific type of grapevine, such as Chardonnay, for example.

# Wine Glossary (con't)

**VERAISON** - The beginning of ripening. An occurrence in unripe grapes when they turn from green to purple, or in the case of white varieties, from green to translucent green, yellow or gold. This is also the time when sugar content begins to increase. Veraison is a point in time from which the time of harvest can be predicted with some accuracy.

**VINIFICATION** - The process of producing wine from grapes; winemaking.

**VINTAGE** - A word with several meanings. The most widely understood meaning applies to the picking of grapes at harvest and making wine with those grapes. Thus, a vintage wine is one that is produced in a particular year.

**VINTNER** - In the U.S., vintner has come to mean the principal of a winery, especially if that person is involved to one degree or another in the winemaking process.

**VITICULTURE** - The science and practice of growing grapes.

**Courtesy of Napa Valley
Vintners Association**

# INDEX

## A

## B

# C

# D

# E

# F

# G

# H

# I

# J

# K

# L

# M

# Q

# R

# T

# V

# W

# Z

**COMPUTOR CONSULTANT:** John H. Welsch

**FRONT COVER:** Bonnie Kezer, ASID of Bonnie Kezer Interior Design

**WINE GLOSSARY:** Napa Valley Vintners Association

**LITERARY COMMENTS:** Colleen O'Brien

**PASTE UP:** Marilyn Kirkwood

**PRINTING:** Publishers Press, Inc.

**PROOFREADING:** Anne Witzleben and
Colleen O'Brien

*For comments, re-orders, the address of your nearest distributor, or information on starting a restaurant guide for your city, please contact:*

**The Tastes of Tahoe**
**P. O. Box 6114**
**Incline Village, Nv. 89450**
**(702)831-5182**

THE TASTES OF TAHOE
P. O. BOX 6114
INCLINE VILLAGE, NV. 89450
(702)831-5182

Please send_____copies of THE TASTES OF TAHOE 1
        at $6.95 each.
Please send_____copies of THE TASTES OF TAHOE 11
        at $7.95 each.
Please send_____copies of THE TASTES OF RENO
        at $6.95 each.
Please send_____copies of THE TASTES OF MARIN
        at $7.95 each.
Please send_____copies of THE TASTES OF CALIFORNIA
        WINE COUNTRY - NAPA/SONOMA at $9.95 each.
Please send_____copies of THE TASTES OF CALIFORNIA
        WINE COUNTRY - NORTH COAST at $9.95 each.
Please send_____copies of COOKING INN STYLE
        at $9.95 each.
Please send_____copies of THE BEST OF THE TASTES OF
        TAHOE at $11.95 each.

Add $1.50 postage and handling for the first book ordered and $.50 for each additional book. Enclosed is my check for $_____

Name_____

Address_____

City_____State__Zip____

This is a gift. Send directly to:
Name_____
Address_____
City_____State__Zip____
Autographed by author.

Autographed to:_____